THE ULTIMATE BIOGRAPHY OF EARTH

NICK LUND ★ ILLUSTRATED BY JASON FORD

WORKMAN PUBLISHING COMPANY ★ NEW YORK

FOR ELLIOTT
—N. L.

LIBRARY OF CONGRESS CATALOGING-IN-PUBLICATION DATA IS AVAILABLE.

ISBN 978-1-5235-1359-8

DESIGN BY SARA CORBETT
COVER ILLUSTRATION BY JASON FORD

WORKMAN BOOKS ARE AVAILABLE AT SPECIAL DISCOUNTS WHEN PURCHASED IN BULK FOR PREMIUMS AND SALES PROMOTIONS AS WELL AS FOR FUNDRAISING OR EDUCATIONAL USE. SPECIAL EDITIONS OR BOOK EXCERPTS CAN ALSO BE CREATED TO SPECIFICATION. FOR DETAILS, CONTACT THE SPECIAL SALES DIRECTOR AT SPECIALMARKETS@WORKMAN.COM.

WORKMAN PUBLISHING CO., INC.
225 VARICK STREET
NEW YORK, NY 10014-4381
WORKMAN.COM

WORKMAN IS A REGISTERED TRADEMARK OF WORKMAN PUBLISHING CO., INC.

PRINTED IN THE USA ON RESPONSIBLY SOURCED PAPER

FIRST PRINTING FEBRUARY 2022

10 9 8 7 6 5 4 3 2 1

CONTENTS

THE BIG BANG!
FORMATION OF THE EARTH

4,600 MILLION YEARS AGO

600 MILLION YEARS

HADEAN EON

PROTEROZOIC EON

1,959 MILLION YEARS

Since this book covers the entire history of Earth, from the Big Bang to Today, we've included this handy timeline to help you follow all 4.5 billion years! You'll also find a marker as each chapter begins so you can keep your place in time as you read. Scientists break history up into different sections of different lengths to keep track of it all. Eons are the largest sections, often covering more than a billion years. And they're divided into smaller measurements of time: eras, periods, epochs, and ages. Scientists use different events

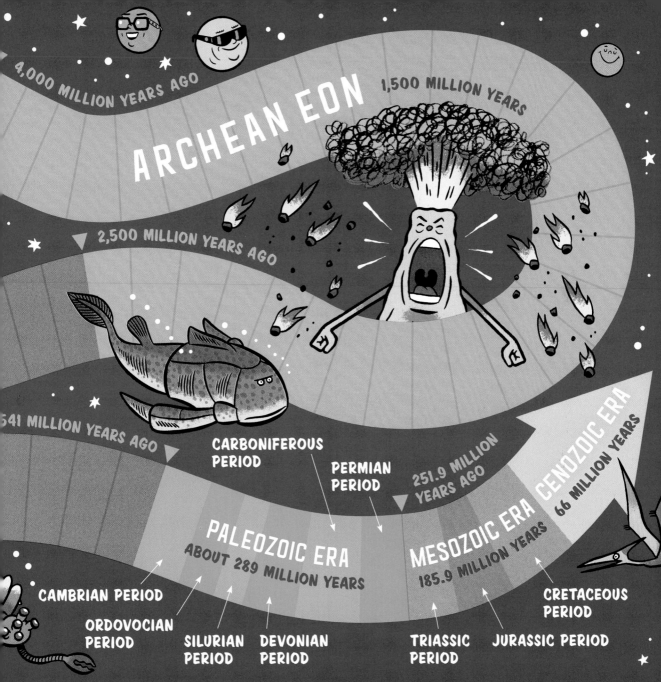

ARCHEAN EON

4,000 MILLION YEARS AGO

1,500 MILLION YEARS

2,500 MILLION YEARS AGO

541 MILLION YEARS AGO

CARBONIFEROUS PERIOD

PERMIAN PERIOD

251.9 MILLION YEARS AGO

66 MILLION YEARS

PALEOZOIC ERA
ABOUT 289 MILLION YEARS

MESOZOIC ERA
185.9 MILLION YEARS

CENOZOIC ERA

CAMBRIAN PERIOD

ORDOVOCIAN PERIOD

SILURIAN PERIOD

DEVONIAN PERIOD

TRIASSIC PERIOD

JURASSIC PERIOD

CRETACEOUS PERIOD

to decide where one unit of time—an eon, era, period, epoch, or age—ends and another begins. Mass extinction, the appearance of a new kind of life, or a change in the chemical makeup of the air are some examples. Because scientists generally know more about what happened in recent history, their study of recent history can be broken into smaller periods of time. That's why the chapters at the beginning of this book generally cover longer time periods than the chapters at the end.

Okay, test, test. Recording session and interview with Earth for use in *The Ultimate Biography*. Actually, before we get started, Earth, I just want to tell you how excited I am to meet you and, you know...to live on you. As a pencil I was literally born to write—but I never thought I'd get to write *your* biography!

It's great to meet you, too, Pencil! But isn't it a bit silly for someone as young as me to have a biography written about them?

Uh...you're four and a half billion years old.

I know! I'm just getting started! I hope there's enough to fill a book.

Right. Well...I think we can fill *one* book.

You're the boss! I'm just worried that I'm not a very good storyteller. How do you help readers feel like they're really *living* my stories? Roaring with the mammoth beasts, bursting with joy at the spontaneous creations, breathing fire with volcanic explosions, running from asteroid collisions—see? There's a lot of action!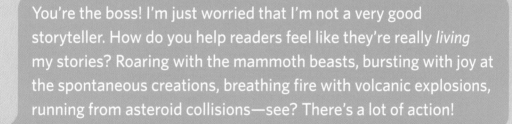

Ah, well, that's where I come in. As the writer, I'll capture every detail for your audience.

I hope you're ready for this. Where should we begin?

At the very beginning, of course.

CHAPTER 1

THE VERY BEGINNING

The Formation of Earth through the Hadean Eon

YOU ARE HERE

I wasn't aware of what was happening during the *early* early times when I was still forming, so I'll just tell you what I've heard.

Who did you hear about your history from?

Human scientists, actually. They're the only ones who've actually studied me. It's been a huge help!

FORMATION OF THE EARTH

First, there was the universe. When it expanded about 13.8 billion years ago, it was very hot and very small, and then it just started growing and growing, and it hasn't stopped. Humans have called the beginning the Big Bang. But no one was around to witness it, so we don't know if it was an actual *Bang!* like an explosion or just gradual growth.

As the universe grew, it cooled down, and *stuff* started to form. Tiny bits of *stuff*, including elements that are still around today, like hydrogen and helium. Massive clouds of those elements and others began forming in space inside the universe. Gravity held the clouds together and pulled the *stuff* toward the middle.

EXPLAINED! UNIVERSE

Earth talks pretty fast and sometimes uses words I don't know. But I look them up later, and I'll share what I discovered in these boxes. The first word is a big one: **universe**. The universe is EVERYTHING. Every single star, planet, and asteroid and all the space, rocks, energy, and every single other thing that exists all around you is the universe. Scientists don't know what's outside the universe, or even if there *is* an outside of the universe.

All that *stuff* collected in the middle of one of those big clouds and got closer and closer and hotter and hotter until it collapsed in on itself in a massive implosion, about 4.7 billion years ago. Gravity spun all that *stuff* together, faster and faster, until there was a new star burning bright at the center: the Sun.

The Sun is millions of massive explosions happening every second. The Sun's *wild*. You'd like her. I mean, if you could meet her without burning up from the heat of her massive, constant explosions, you know? She's so cool.

After the Sun was created, there was still a lot of that *stuff* cloud around. It looked sort of like a Frisbee shape around the Sun, and it was filled with tiny atoms of elements.

EXPLAINED! ATOMS + ELEMENTS

In the same way that different ingredients are mixed together to make food—pizza is made from water, yeast, flour, salt, tomato sauce, pepperoni, and delicious, delicious cheese—**atoms** are the ingredients that go together to make *stuff*. Atoms are incredibly tiny, hundreds of thousands of times smaller than a human hair, but they combine to make all of the *stuff* in the universe. Scientists have identified 118 different kinds of atoms, and each different kind is called an **element**. Elements on Earth include oxygen, gold, carbon, and something called—I'm not kidding—rutherfordium. We keep track of the elements on a big, colorful chart called the periodic table of the elements, which helps us understand how elements are grouped and how they relate to one another.

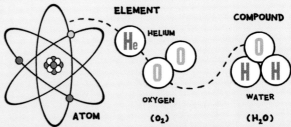

ELEMENT

H_e HELIUM

COMPOUND

ATOM

OXYGEN (O_2)

WATER (H_2O)

Gravity began to cause all those little atoms floating around the Sun to smash together. Slowly they began to form larger and larger clumps of *stuff*. Those clumps would occasionally smash into one another, causing them to grow and to form new clumps. These clumps kept spinning and smashing for millions of years until they became four distinct planets orbiting the Sun: Mercury, Venus, Mars, and a very young baby Earth.

Four other planets formed farther away from the Sun, where it's colder: Jupiter, Saturn, Uranus, and Neptune. Somewhere out there in the universe there is a line called the frost line. This is where water and other compounds stay frozen solid. Those solid clumps of *stuff* beyond the frost line built up into huge planets that are massive and cold and also pretty gassy. (Hydrogen-and-helium gassy, that is. Not bean gassy.) Pluto is out there, too.

These planets might just fly out into space, but the Sun's gravity holds them in place, spinning around in what's called an orbit. If you were to swing a yo-yo on a string around your head, the forward movement of the yo-yo keeps it from falling, and the string (gravity) keeps it from flying away—that's an orbit. The Sun's gravity holds not just the eight planets in orbit but also thousands of smaller things, like comets, dwarf planets, moons, and other objects.

I'M THE SMALLEST PLANET AND THE CLOSEST TO THE SUN, WHICH MEANS I GET REALLY HOT DURING THE DAY BUT REALLY REALLY *BRRRRR* COLD AT NIGHT.
I'M THE HOTTEST PLANET IN THE SOLAR SYSTEM, WHICH MEANS MY SURFACE IS MOSTLY DESERT, AND I'M COVERED IN THICK CLOUDS OF ROTTEN-SMELLING GAS.
THAT'S ME!
MERCURY
VENUS
EARTH
BACK IN THE DAY I USED TO HAVE HUGE OCEANS OF WATER, BUT NOW MY COOLEST FEATURE IS OLYMPUS MONS, THE LARGEST MOUNTAIN IN THE SOLAR SYSTEM.

So Earth was formed about 4.5 billion years ago. Things were pretty rough for the first 600 million years. Those big clumps of *stuff* left over from when the Sun formed were still constantly smashing into the young Earth. It was chaotic, but all that space *stuff* added to the size of the young planet.

As Earth grew, it got hotter. Soon it was so hot that most of the rocks and metals that made up Earth melted. Metals like iron and nickel sank deep into the center and became a solid metal core. The rest of Earth was made up of hot liquid rock, or magma, and the surface was a thin crust of cooler rock. Very similar to the way Earth is structured now.

The solid metal center and liquid magma inside the spinning Earth created a magnetic field around the planet. See, one crucial ingredient needed before any life could develop was something called an atmosphere. This is a bunch of gases trapped by gravity in a layer around the planet. Gases like oxygen, carbon dioxide, and nitrogen are necessary for living things to breathe and for plants to grow. Earth's magnetic field works as a sort of shield, protecting it from solar winds that would otherwise blow the atmosphere away and make it impossible for any life to form or survive. That's what happened on Mars, actually. It once had flowing water 3 billion years ago before solar winds stripped away the planet's atmosphere.

EXPLAINED! GRAVITY

Gravity is a natural force that brings two things together. If there are two things floating in space, gravity pulls them toward each other. Gravity is what keeps the Moon orbiting around Earth and Earth orbiting around the Sun. When you throw a ball, gravity is the force that brings it back to Earth instead of allowing it to fly out into space. When you jump, gravity brings you back down to the ground. Gravity is what keeps everything on Earth from flying off into space, and life as we know it could not exist without it.

There were still lots of clumps of *stuff* floating around and smashing into Earth all the time. The biggest clump was Theia. It was about the size of Mars—and it came flying in and slammed into Earth straight on. *BAM!* This was about 4.4 billion years ago. The crash created huge oceans of hot liquid rock on Earth's surface, as well as a band of debris that began circling the planet, sort of like the rings of Saturn. It was intense. All that debris spun around and around until it collected into a single body: the Moon.

> Even though she's far away, I feel like the Moon is always near. She's the brightest object in the sky—more than 14,000 times brighter than Venus, which is the second brightest. And what would nights on Earth be without the Moon shining in the sky? Weird, that's what.

The Moon and the Earth have a close relationship. Earth's gravity keeps the Moon orbiting around it, so the Moon doesn't float away into space. The Moon has its own gravity, too, and it pulls on the Earth. The Moon's

gravity affects the Earth's oceans, pulling them back and forth across the planet. The daily rising and falling of the ocean caused by the Moon's gravity is called tides, and the constant movement of all that water circulates food for all kinds of animals.

> You sure got knocked around a lot as you were growing, Earth!

> Yeah, they were wild times. Your scientists call my earliest years the Hadean eon, because I looked sort of like Hades, the ancient Greeks' name for the underworld and the god who ruled it.

> Your earliest years were named after the god of the dead? But . . . you're where life exists!

> I *am* where life exists! Let's keep going.

Earth's surface was a terrible place to be at that time. There was still a lot of *stuff* floating around the solar system, and as it approached the Earth, Earth's gravity could pull it in. Comets, meteoroids, asteroids, and other dangerous space rocks were constantly smashing into Earth and causing huge, fiery explosions, which made things very, very hot.

EXPLAINED! SPACE ROCKS

Scientists have different names for different kinds of floating space rocks. **Comets** are big, sometimes miles wide, and are mostly made of ice and dust. They orbit the Sun, and so the same comet can be seen repeatedly, like the famous Halley's Comet, which buzzes by Earth every 75 years. **Asteroids** are also very large, like comets, but are made out of rock and metal instead of ice. Comets and asteroids rarely hit Earth anymore, but when they do, they can cause massive damage, like the asteroid 66 million years ago that ended the Age of the Dinosaurs (see page 138). **Meteoroids** are the size of a small boulder or a grain of sand. They float around space and sometimes fall to Earth. Meteoroids often vaporize when they enter Earth's atmosphere. This creates **meteors**, or "shooting stars." When a meteoroid doesn't vaporize and instead falls to Earth as a space rock, it's called a **meteorite**. It's estimated that more than a dozen meteorites hit Earth every day, but they're mostly too small for anyone to notice.

It was so hot that there wasn't much of that all-important substance that makes all things possible on Earth: water.

Earth was too hot in its earliest days for water to form, but it eventually got there. The key was in some of those comets and asteroids that kept walloping the planet: many of them were made of ice, which deposited some water onto Earth's surface.

Earth is really lucky to be where it is in the lineup of planets. If it were closer to the Sun, it would lose all of its water to the heat. But if it were much farther away, everything would be permanently frozen. So it's in the perfect spot to have luscious, flowing oceans of water covering more than 70 percent of its surface. And with water, came LIFE!

EXPLAINED! WATER

Water is formed when two atoms of hydrogen bond with one atom of oxygen. Pure water is tasteless, odorless, and colorless. It's the only substance on Earth commonly found in all three states: solid (ice), liquid (water), and gas (steam). Water makes up the majority of our bodies and those of most living things, as well as much of the atmosphere and the Earth's surface.

Water is important, because without it I wouldn't have the most unique thing about me. Living things!

YOU
ARE
HERE

CHAPTER 2

LIFE HAS EVOLVED, AND IT ITCHES

The Archean Eon

> Wow, look at these gorgeous mountains!

 Hmm, mountains. Too itchy.

> …Itchy?

 Yeah, every time a new mountain range is created on my surface it itches like crazy and I can't ever scratch it! Plus, the first life evolves during the Archean and that itches, too. Being a planet isn't easy!

FORMATION OF THE EARTH

CENOZOIC ERA

MESOZOIC ERA   PALEOZOIC ERA

Earth was still extremely hot back then. But pretty soon after the whole Moon explosion, the oceans of molten rock on Earth's surface cooled into a solid crust around the outside. You can think of it sort of like an egg: a thin shell covering a whole lot of liquid. Earth has a thin crust of cooled rock that protects everything on it—oceans, trees, animals—from falling into a bath of molten rock.

Scientists call the solid outer crust, including the surface of the Earth where we are, the lithosphere. It sort of surfs on top of a less-solid-but-not-really-liquid mass of rock called the asthenosphere.

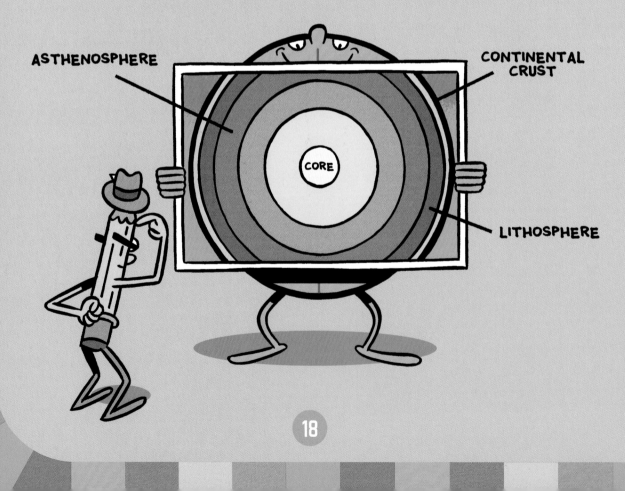

ASTHENOSPHERE

CONTINENTAL CRUST

CORE

LITHOSPHERE

The boundary between the solid crust and the not-so-solid part isn't constant, and it's anywhere from about 25 miles (40.2 km) to 175 miles (281.6 km) below the surface. There are pockets of molten rock, or magma, down under the crust, and they sometimes make it up to the surface through volcanoes.

EXPLAINED! MOLTEN ROCK

When rocks get superheated, they melt and become a hot, gooey, burning, thick, liquid molten rock. When that **molten rock** is underground, it's called magma. When the magma makes it to the Earth's surface, usually from a volcano, it becomes lava. When lava cools, it becomes solid rock once again.

There is something very important about the lithosphere, Earth's solid outer crust: it's not one whole shell. Instead, it's broken up into a whole bunch of huge, heavy pieces called tectonic plates. These plates float around on the softer, not-so-solid asthenosphere. The plates touch one another, but each of them moves around separately—very, very slowly, but separately. And where they rub up against one another, crazy things can happen.

One thing that happens when two plates meet is that huge mountains form. Most of the time, one of the plates slides down under the other plate, pushing it up. Current mountain ranges like the South American Andes and the North American Cascade Range formed at the intersection of tectonic plates, just in the past 30 million years or so. Over Earth's long history, many mountain ranges have risen up and been eroded down, lost forever.

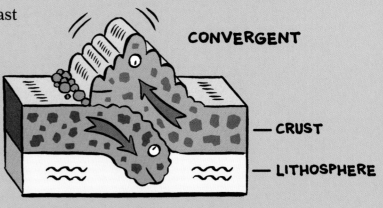

CONVERGENT

— CRUST

— LITHOSPHERE

On the border of India and Nepal, the Indian Plate and the Eurasian Plate have been smashing into each other for the past 50 million years, each pushing the other upward to form the Himalayan Mountains. One of those mountains, Mount Everest, is currently the tallest mountain on Earth's surface, and the range is still growing at a rate of one inch (2.5 cm) or so per year.

Another thing that happens when two tectonic plates meet is earthquakes. As two plates slide past each other, they sometimes get caught, and pressure builds. When the plates finally move, the sudden release of pressure causes an earthquake. This movement sends waves of energy through the surrounding rock. Just like waves on the ocean, these waves of energy flow through the Earth's crust, shaking and rattling everything in their path.

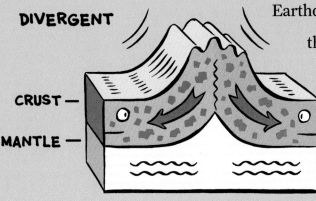

DIVERGENT

CRUST —

MANTLE —

Earthquakes can happen anywhere, but they're much more common along the areas where two tectonic plates meet.

Volcanoes are also common at the boundaries of tectonic plates. But instead of the two plates smashing into each other like they do to form a mountain, these two plates are pulling apart. A lot of energy is generated from plates moving, and that energy turns to heat, which melts some of the rock in the asthenosphere below. That creates a bunch of hot magma, and it rises to fill the area left open by the two plates splitting apart. The pressure builds and builds and . . . *BAHGOOOOOOSH!* There is an explosion.

Volcanoes are a constant presence on Earth's surface, and they always have been. Volcanoes can occur on land or under the ocean. When undersea volcanoes occur close to

the ocean's surface, the result is often the creation of islands from all of the new rock coming from the eruption. The country of Iceland was formed this way, and it's still volcanically active. Volcanoes also create much of the seafloor. Huge eruptions—and every few million years there are some really, really huge eruptions—can change worldwide weather patterns, with massive consequences for life around the world. The Siberian Traps eruptions lasted for 2 million years and contributed to the biggest extinction of life in Earth's history (see page 104). Volcanic eruptions also transport water from the Earth's mantle into the atmosphere. During the Archean eon, they helped form the massive oceans around Earth's surface.

The next thing you need to know about are continents. Continents are large areas of land. Scientists aren't exactly sure how the first continents formed or what they looked like. But they think it might have to do with the fact that the rocks that make up continents, or continental crust, are less dense than the rocks that make up oceanic crust. That means the lighter crust rose to the top during all the pulling and smashing of tectonic plates, leaving large land continents high and dry.

Today, there are considered to be seven continents on Earth—Africa, Antarctica, Asia, Australia, Europe, North America, and South America.

But it wasn't always that way. Not even close. In the billions of years of Earth's history, we've seen continents come and go. Huge ones broke apart, and their pieces floated away only to smash into one another and form new landmasses.

As often happens when plates and continents slide into one another, one plate is pushed under, and that rock is melted back into the asthenosphere. After billions of years of that happening over and over all around the world, there's very little rock from the oldest continents left on Earth's surface, except for some rocks in western Australia.

Scientists still haven't quite figured out what exactly the first continent looked like or what parts of it are still around, but they have two guesses. Some scientists have noticed similarities between the rocks in the Pilbara Craton in Australia and those in southern Africa. They believe that these two cratons (a fancy word for "very old parts of continents") were once part of the same continent, which existed around 3.6 billion years ago and which they've named Vaalbara.

The other theory is that the still-existing Australian rocks were joined with some other still-existing rocks in southern Africa and in India to make a small, early continent called Ur. No one really knows for sure. And it's important to remember that the majority of Earth's surface at this point was ocean.

Sometimes there are layers in the rock where your scientists find fossils. That's life, my most amazing feature!

It . . . doesn't look very lifelike to me.

Life isn't all dinosaurs and daffodils. It started very simply.

No one is exactly sure how life on Earth began, but it's one of the most important questions in all of science. How did life begin? Scientists have a lot of theories, the most likely being that life began out of combinations of nonliving  chemicals. Different chemicals are constantly connecting and reacting to one another in nature, and somewhere, some combination of chemicals and minerals and heat and water and elements produced the first life.

Scientists aren't really sure where the first life occurred. It could have happened around deep-sea volcanic vents pretty soon after the Earth was formed, in the Hadean eon, 4.5 billion years ago. Or it might have happened on land in the Archean eon. Some scientists have found evidence of life about 3.5 billion years old in rocks in Greenland and

Australia. It's really hard to know for sure when things are that old, but scientists are making new discoveries all the time.

Life began with tiny, single-celled microorganisms. (For comparison, your human body is estimated to be made up of about 40 *trillion* cells.) These earliest cells, called prokaryotes, were simple compared to all the life-forms that have evolved from them. But they were the most complex thing on Earth at that time.

EXPLAINED! CELLS

Cells are the fundamental building blocks of life.

Each cell is like a small factory working to fulfill its role in a living thing. The nucleus is the boss, and it contains information telling the cell what to make and how. A wall, called a membrane, keeps everything inside. The rest of the cell is filled with structures that work to make the products—proteins, acids, or other things—or move materials in or out. Working together, the cell factory completes its tasks, and life goes on. Living things contain many different kinds of cells, each with certain roles to play. Some roles, such as taking in energy and using it to grow, are shared by all cells. Other roles are just for certain cells. For example, the role of a bone cell is to be as strong as possible, while the role of a brain cell is to carry messages to different parts of the body. Different kinds of cells working together create all the complexity of life.

Is there anything you remember about the first time life emerged?

Yep! I remember it was itchy.

Well, I'll explain…

Back in the Archean, some of those single-celled organisms, called microbes, started sort of hanging out and joining together to form thin mats. Each type of microbe would "feed" on a certain chemical—for example, a chemical called sulfate—and turn it into a waste chemical, in this case sulfite, that could be "eaten" by another kind of microbe. This produced a sort of food chain.

The top layers of these microbial mats were occupied by special microbes that could get fuel from the sun through a special process called photosynthesis. These microbes used energy from sunlight to break down water molecules into hydrogen, oxygen, and electrons, which are then combined with a chemical called carbon dioxide to produce sugars that the microbes can use for fuel.

The development of photosynthesis was a huge milestone for life on Earth for two reasons. First, since there's so much sunlight, water, and carbon dioxide on Earth, life-forms that were able to get energy from those things could live almost anywhere, including, eventually, on land. Second, one of the chemicals left over from breaking down water was oxygen, which these photosynthetic microbes began releasing into Earth's atmosphere in large quantities. And eventually, all that oxygen could be used by lots of other living things.

Many of these microbial mats lived at the edge of the sea, where they got their energy from the sun and the water. The cells stopped themselves from being washed away by binding with the sand and eventually formed layers of "living rock" called stromatolites. Some of those stromatolites eventually became fossils in what is now Australia, and scientists discovered them as evidence of life during the Archean!

EXPLAINED! FOSSILS

A **fossil** is the preserved remains of a very old thing. Fossils are made in many different ways. For example, if a fly falls into some mud, then the mud dries out and turns to stone, the fly is preserved inside. Or the fly could get caught in some tree sap, which then hardens into amber with the fly locked inside. Or the fly could fall into some mud again, and his body dissolves away, leaving just the imprint of the fly on the stone. Each of these is a fossil. Fossils have taught us almost everything we know about ancient life.

CHAPTER 3

A BREATH OF FRESH AIR

The Proterozoic Eon

YOU ARE HERE

> Look, it's a snowball Earth, Pencil! I'm almost completely covered in snow and ice. Everything's so beautiful, so peaceful, isn't it?

> Easy for you to say, what with your hot molten insides keeping you warm. Can a pencil get a jacket around here, please? Maybe some hot cocoa?

> Well, how about we just get started.

FORMATION OF THE EARTH

Oxygen is a really important element. It's required to make water, and without oxygen, it's unlikely that much life beyond those prokaryotes would have ever evolved. There's a lot of oxygen on Earth today—it's one of the most abundant elements in the whole universe. But back at the end of the Archean, there just wasn't much of it around. One thing about oxygen is that it likes to combine with other elements and form new things. Almost all of the oxygen that was floating around early in Earth's history was combining with other elements and disappearing from Earth's surface. That is, until the oxygen factories came along.

All living things need energy to live. (*You* get your energy from food.) New cells, called cyanobacteria, got their energy by mixing sunlight, water, and carbon dioxide. When they were done with all that mixing, the cells had something left over that they didn't need: oxygen, which they released into the air. So once cyanobacteria evolved and started to spread, oxygen started to exist in the atmosphere.

But for the longest time, all that new oxygen didn't really stay in the atmosphere. Remember that oxygen likes to combine with other things, right? Well, some of those things are elements like carbon, iron, and sulfur. There was a lot of carbon, iron, and sulfur around when cyanobacteria started doing their thing, so for about 500 million years, all the new oxygen went and combined with those elements instead of building up in the atmosphere.

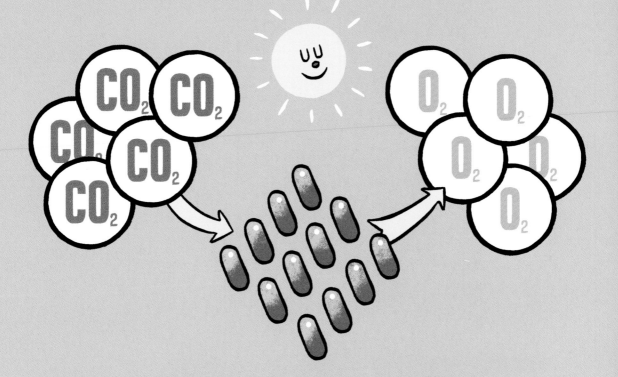

But cyanobacteria kept growing and growing and producing more and more oxygen, which was combining with other elements until, well, it wasn't anymore. About 2.5 billion years ago, oxygen had combined with almost all of the things it was going to combine with, and so the rest just started filling the atmosphere. The atmosphere was changing. Scientists call this time the Great Oxygenation Event! And with that, the Proterozoic eon began.

ORIENTATION OF THE EARTH

The Earth is round, which means that, as it spins, one part of it is closest to the Sun. That part is called the **equator**. Because the equator is closest to the Sun, it's typically hotter there than on any other part of Earth. The very top and bottom of the Earth, called the **North** and **South Poles**, stay farther away from the Sun throughout the days and years, so they are colder. The North and South Poles aren't straight up and down; rather, the Earth leans slightly. So as the Earth orbits the Sun, each half of Earth is tipped a little bit toward the Sun for part of the year (making things a little warmer in summer) and tipped away for the other part (making things a little colder in winter). The tilt gives us seasons!

EARTH'S TILT
23.5°

NORTH POLE

TROPIC OF CANCER

EQUATOR

SOUTH POLE

TROPIC OF CAPRICORN

Before the Great Oxygenation Event, there was a lot of a chemical called methane in Earth's atmosphere. The methane was put there by single-celled organisms that had been releasing it as a waste product since the Archean. One thing about an atmosphere with a lot of methane is that it's really warm because methane doesn't let heat escape. (In fact, a global increase in methane emissions is contributing to a warming climate in the present day.) During the Great Oxygenation Event, cyanobacteria showed up and started to produce all that oxygen, which combined with the methane to form water and carbon dioxide. The heat-trapping methane in the atmosphere was reduced, Earth's temperature plummeted, and the planet became a snowball.

The global freeze and the influx of oxygen into the atmosphere weren't great for a lot of the life on Earth. There were a lot of oxygen-loving cyanobacteria around, but most of the living prokaryotes weren't used to so much oxygen, and it was toxic to them. The Great Oxygenation Event made way for the Huronian glaciation, which was actually pretty catastrophic for life on Earth, and much of it died.

> There have actually been quite a few periods in my history where a lot of things died. But each and every time life survives—somewhere, somehow.

It's thought that the extinctions caused by the Great Oxygenation Event and the Huronian glaciation killed off much of the single-celled life on Earth, but they opened the door to more complicated cells, as well as to multicelled organisms.

EXPLAINED! EXTINCTION

When all individuals of a particular type of living thing have died, that creature is **extinct**. Many species have gone extinct over Earth's long history. In fact, scientists estimate that 99 percent of all species that ever lived are now extinct. Species die out for many reasons, including things like a drastic change to their environment (like from a huge asteroid impact) or being pushed out by other animals. Humans can also cause a species to go extinct by destroying natural areas, overfishing and overhunting, or polluting the environment. (See page 158.)

New kinds of cells, called eukaryotes, evolved, and these cells would go on to make up animals and plants. Eukaryotes are much bigger than prokaryotes—up to 10,000 times bigger. They are filled with fancy elements, like a nucleus, which contains genetic material, mitochondria to provide the cell with energy, and various internal membranes to keep the different parts from messing one another up. All this organization meant that eukaryotic cells could do a lot more, and in the billions of years since, they have helped create every plant and animal on Earth.

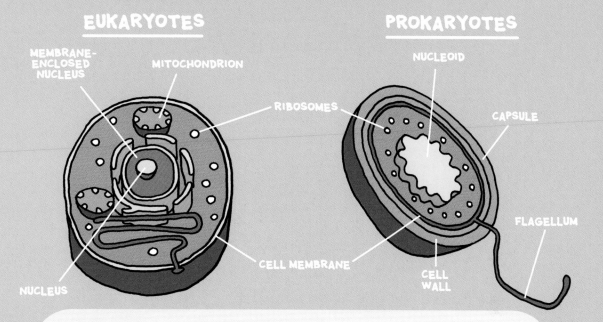

EUKARYOTES

MEMBRANE-ENCLOSED NUCLEUS

MITOCHONDRION

RIBOSOMES

NUCLEUS

CELL MEMBRANE

PROKARYOTES

NUCLEOID

CAPSULE

FLAGELLUM

CELL WALL

EXPLAINED! GENES

Genes are the set of instructions for building life-forms. They're made up of molecules called DNA, which is basically a code that is read by other cells and tells them how to form. Genes are passed on from one generation to the next. In single-celled organisms, the cell makes an exact copy of its own DNA and then splits its body in half, making two cells that are exactly the same. (That is, unless there are mutations in the genes, which happens all the time.) Humans pass on their genes by having babies, and each parent gives half of their DNA to their child.

Eukaryotes flourished during the middle of the Proterozoic, a time when things were fairly calm and life was still so new. Some of them started to join together to form multicellular organisms. Though the majority of life on Earth at this time was still single-celled microorganisms (in fact, prokaryotes still outnumber eukaryotes today), lots of different things began to show up. Tons of those stromatolites formed from all kinds of different layers of bacteria. And by the end of the Proterozoic, multicellular life had combined to form the ancestors of what we know now as fungi, plants, and even animals!

So no huge animals in the Proterozoic, huh.

Nope, things happened very slowly back in my early eons. Everything was just getting started. In fact, scientists jokingly call a big chunk of the Proterozoic "the Boring Billion" because not much happened.

The Boring Billion! That must have been a rough stretch for you.

It was relaxing, actually! I'd take a "Boring Billion" over a "Being-Smashed-by-a-Floating-Planetoid-and-Blasting-Molten-Rock-Into-Space-to-Create-the-Moon Billion" any day. There was lots of excitement to come and something of an explosion of life during our next stop, the Cambrian!

CHAPTER 4

AN EXPLOSION! BUT THE GOOD KIND

The Cambrian Period

All right, the Cambrian period was an absolutely wild time!

Wow, we went from tiny little mats of microbes to enough sea creatures to fill a whole aquarium!

That's right, it was an explosion of life. The Cambrian Explosion!

FORMATION OF THE EARTH

CENOZOIC ERA

MESOZOIC ERA   PALEOZOIC ERA

YOU ARE HERE

The Cambrian period began about 541 million years in the past. This was a shorter period of time than anything we've covered so far. The Hadean, Archean, and Proterozoic eons covered hundreds of millions or billions of years. But from this point on, Earth's timeline is broken down into shorter periods because tons of interesting things were happening, and scientists have learned a lot more about them.

During the Archean and Proterozoic, big continents were still drifting around smashing into one another and splitting apart. First there was Kenorland, which then became Arctica, then Atlantica, then Columbia, then Rodinia, and now Pannotia.

At the start of the Cambrian, Pannotia was the biggest continent around, but it wasn't the only one: Baltica, Siberia, and others were also close by, though they were much smaller.

But Pannotia didn't stick around forever. The slow but steady movement of tectonic plates was causing it to break apart just as the Cambrian period was beginning. Two huge landmasses called Gondwana and Laurentia split off and were drifting away from each other, leaving a new area of water called the Iapetus Ocean between them. Though it may seem like it happened quickly, it took millions of years for these continents to drift apart. Continents drifted then—and still drift today—at about the same speed as your fingernails grow!

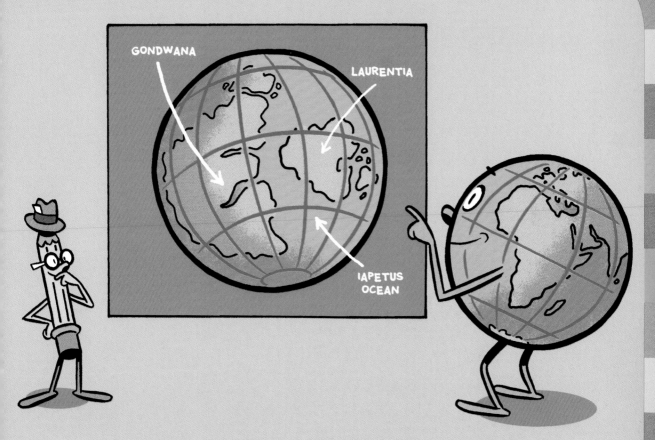

There wasn't a whole lot of anything happening on land during the Cambrian. No plants yet. But there were some more microbial mats in the tidal areas. And a few slug-like animals dragging themselves around on mud flats. But there was a lot of excitement happening underwater.

The Cambrian Explosion produced uncountable new species, including the beginnings of the major groups of modern animals, in just 10 or 20 million years. These creatures represent just some of the life that evolved during this period over the course of 55 million years. The earliest representatives of almost all major groups of animals developed during the Cambrian.

The seafloor was covered in those microbial mats, big concentrations of single-celled organisms. Late in the Proterozoic, multicelled organisms like tiny worms came along to start snacking on these microbial mats, and they burrowed down through the mats and into the mud below, helping to release nutrients back into the ocean for the benefit of other animals. Scientists have found fossils of lots of these old burrows in the mud.

Trilobites were another multicelled organism crawling all around on the seafloor. They're not around anymore, but their ability to live in a variety of conditions helped them become one of the most successful creatures in Earth's whole history, having lived for more than 250 million years. Because they were so widespread and had a hard outer skeleton that was easily fossilized, tons of trilobite fossils are found in different parts of the world today.

EXPLAINED! **TAXONOMY**

There are lots and lots and lots of living things, and scientists need a way to keep track of them all. So scientists organize the relationships living things have to one another using **taxonomy**. It's set up so that each animal is in a big upside-down pyramid, with the category at the top containing the most living things and the category at the bottom containing just one living thing. There are eight levels, or ranks: domain, kingdom, phylum, class, order, family, genus, and species.

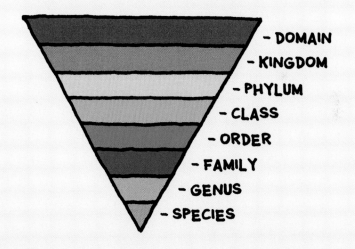

- DOMAIN
- KINGDOM
- PHYLUM
- CLASS
- ORDER
- FAMILY
- GENUS
- SPECIES

There were lots of different kinds of trilobites over their history, and different species lived in different ways—some were bottom-feeders; some were predators; some swam around looking for plankton. They ranged in size from very small to almost two feet (60 cm) long.

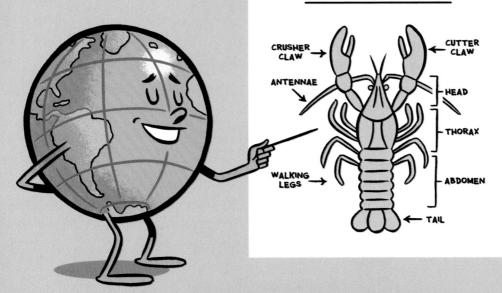

THE AMERICAN LOBSTER

CRUSHER CLAW

CUTTER CLAW

ANTENNAE

HEAD

THORAX

WALKING LEGS

ABDOMEN

TAIL

Trilobites were some of the first of an important group of animals called arthropods. These are animals with an external, protective skeleton and a segmented body. That outer skeleton is an important adaptation because it protects the animal and its inner organs from predators. It also allowed them to survive in many different habitats and temperatures—eventually arthropods were able to leave water and live on land. Arthropods, which include insects, spiders, millipedes, and crabs, are still thriving on Earth, making up approximately 80 percent of all living animal species. Their armored body design was a success, helping arthropods to spread around the world and evolve into many amazing and odd shapes during the Cambrian.

One species of *Marrella*, originally called a lace crab, sort of looks like what would happen if a heavy metal rock band designed a harp.

There were lots of *Marrella* crawling around the seafloor during the Cambrian. They were thought to be scavengers, eating anything that sank to the seafloor. These bottom-feeding creatures and others were important to new cycles of life in the oceans because they helped break down nutrients that fell to the seafloor and return them to other animals when they themselves were eaten.

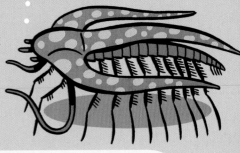

EXPLAINED! PALEONTOLOGY

Paleontology is the scientific study of ancient life. Paleontologists look for and study fossils and examine chemical evidence to piece together how ancient life began and evolved. You can thank a paleontologist for pretty much every fact in this book!

Then there was *Opabinia*. It was about 2 to 3 inches (5 to 7.5 cm) long, a little bigger than *Marrella*, and one of the wildest-looking animals yet! *Opabinia* was likely a carnivore, meaning that it fed on other animals. It probably used its long, hollow nose thing to plunge into the seafloor and capture prey. No one's really sure how it worked, but, man, it looked cool!

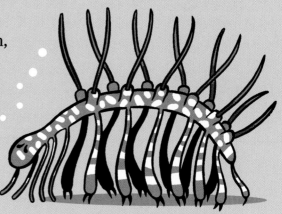

Then there is *Pikaia*, a kind of small eel-like worm that, very importantly, had a nerve cord running down the length of its body. That nerve was a very primitive spinal cord, making *Pikaia* not an arthropod but likely an ancestor of creatures with backbones, like fish and mammals. We'll see plenty of them later.

Hallucigenia, a walking spiny worm, was named that because the scientists who found it thought they were hallucinating—which means seeing things that weren't actually real. Scientists still understand very little about it, but they're pretty sure that it walked around on its little paired legs and had spikes on its back for protection. They also believe it was an ancestor of predatory jungle creatures called velvet worms, which are still alive today.

The spiny little crawling creature is a *Wiwaxia*. *Wiwaxia* had spines, and it also had rows of tiny scales along its back, likely for protection. It crawled along the bottom of the ocean, sort of like a slug, though scientists think that it's probably more closely related to things like clams.

A lot of these tiny animals had spines for protection from creatures like *Anomalocaris*, the top predator of the Cambrian. During a time when most animals were no more than a couple of inches (a few centimeters) long, *Anomalocaris* could grow to more than 3 feet (1 m)! It was like a whale plus a manatee plus a cockroach all rolled into one deadly package. It had amazing eyesight, and unlike most animals at the time, it was able to swim through the water by smoothly waving the flaps on the sides of its body. No one is quite sure what *Anomalocaris* ate—it may have feasted on trilobites, or it may have simply filtered bits of food out of the water, like some whales do—but it was certainly the largest and most fearsome animal that had ever existed up to this point.

There were tons of other things in the oceans, too. Jellyfish were around, and the ones scientists have found look just like some of the jellyfish that are still swimming today. Marine worms existed at this time, too.

49

Because their bodies are entirely soft, you won't see them appear in the fossil record of this time as frequently, but they were there. There were clam-like animals called *Lingula* that still exist and look pretty much the same as they did 500 million years ago.

There are a couple of likely explanations for this burst of new life, all of which are still debated by scientists. First was all that new oxygen coming into the atmosphere at the end of the Proterozoic. The new complex cells needed oxygen to function, and so the additional oxygen that was available in the air or in the water made it possible for animals to grow larger and larger while still getting the oxygen they needed.

Another explanation is that an element called calcium built up in the ocean at the beginning of the Cambrian, either from underwater volcanoes or by washing into the water from continental rocks. Calcium is used by humans to build bones, but Cambrian arthropods used it to build strong outer

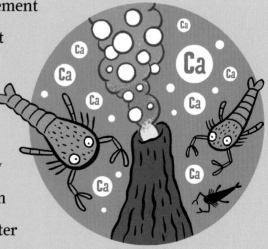

skeletons and other hard body parts, which allowed them to grow bigger and protect themselves. This probably also helped lead to a lot of new creatures.

Finally, there were a lot of new niches for animals to explore at the start of the Cambrian. Different species were able to grow new body types that let them explore different ways to live on the seafloor, such as burrowing into it, grazing on microbial mats, feeding on the things grazing on the mats, and more. Each of these new ways to live allowed a whole bunch of new species to evolve and spread around the globe.

EXPLAINED! EVOLUTION

Evolution is how populations of living things change over time. It's all about reproduction. When animals produce offspring—either by one organism reproducing asexually or by two organisms together reproducing sexually—the parent or parents each pass on their genes to their offspring. Over time, the small changes made from genes passing from parents to offspring can result in drastic changes to the species. This happens when the small changes give the children advantages over their peers, such as making it easier to find food or attract a mate. The slow processes of genetic change and natural selection have resulted in all the different forms of life on Earth.

Life flourished in the Cambrian, but it wasn't all smooth sailing. In fact, the second half of the Cambrian saw mostly a slow decrease in the number of species in the ocean. This eventually resulted in what's known as the Cambrian–Ordovician extinction event. Scientists are still working out what happened, but possible causes include a decrease in the amount of oxygen in the oceans and a global cooling brought on by glaciers forming on continents.

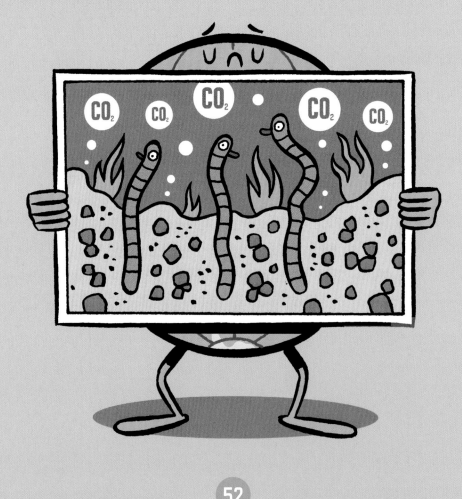

EXPLAINED! SEA LEVELS

The level of the ocean is constantly changing. The most important factor is the shape of the sea bottom. Just like those beneath land continents, the tectonic plates under the sea are in motion. When they spread out, the **sea level** drops. When they rise up, they push the sea upward with them. Global sea levels are also affected by glaciers, which hold water like a sponge and cause sea levels to drop. When glaciers and ice caps melt, the water returns to the seas, causing water levels to rise. Global sea levels are also impacted by water temperature—as the water warms it expands—and by the amount of water in lakes and rivers.

So the Cambrian Explosion kinda fizzled out, huh?

It took millions of years, but yeah. Like I said earlier, lots of living things have come and gone over my history. The good thing is that life always bounces back, better than before. And it did again, in the Ordovician.

CHAPTER 5

THE BIG CHILL

The Ordovician and Silurian Periods

 It didn't take life long to rebound after the extinction at the end of the Cambrian, and soon my oceans were filled with new creatures. And, finally, life was emerging from the water and beginning to creep onto dry land.

Oh, cool, it must have been fun to have so much activity going on!

 Yeah, it was great....Except for that little blip in the middle.

...Blip in the middle?

 Yeah, it was pretty rough. You'll see.

FORMATION OF THE EARTH

CENOZOIC ERA

MESOZOIC ERA   PALEOZOIC ERA

YOU ARE HERE

The beginning of the Ordovician was about 485 million years ago. The Cambrian Explosion had come and gone, and now Earth was primed for another burst of new life.

The Ordovician came in hot, so to speak. Worldwide volcanic activity raised carbon dioxide levels. Today, humans are causing carbon dioxide levels to rise very quickly, but they were even higher then. This kept the Earth's temperature high, with little ice and high sea levels. Much of the dry land was concentrated in a single continent called Gondwana, which was hanging out near the equator but was slowly drifting south. A few other, smaller continents—Laurentia, Baltica, and Siberia—were around, too, but they were comparatively small islands due to the high sea levels.

Conditions were improving. The lack of oxygen that killed

so many species in the second half of the Cambrian reversed. Scientists aren't exactly sure how, but things were just kinda nice and warm. A bunch of volcanic activity and tectonic plates rubbing up against one another flooded the seas with nutrients like phosphorus and potassium. These factors probably drove an increase in the amount of plankton—tiny, floating organisms in the ocean—which provided an opportunity for things that eat plankton, like sea urchins and sea lilies, to grow and for the things that eat the things that eat plankton, like large, shelled nautiloids, to grow, too.

So the life-forms that survived the Cambrian found themselves with a lot of new food, and high sea levels flooded previously dry areas, which gave sea creatures new areas to explore. All this new food and new habitat meant great conditions for new species to evolve. Overall, the number of different kinds of animals in the oceans increased during the Ordovician by 300 percent.

Many of those animals are still with us in one form or another. The cephalopod family was expanding and flourished, eventually giving us creatures like squid and octopuses. The most numerous cephalopods at the time were large, swimming, shelled creatures called nautiloids. There are only a few living nautiloid species today, but there were more than 2,500 different types in the Ordovician.

CHAMBERED NAUTILUS
(NAUTILUS POMPILIUS)

Each of these species of nautilus had a distinct type of large shell and up to 90 tentacles emerging from the open end. These creatures were some of the largest and most formidable predators of the Ordovician seas. They had special organs that allowed them to "smell" chemicals in the water left by their prey, helping them hunt and eat shrimp and other crustaceans. Each nautilus species sported its own unique shell. Some were shaped like cones; some were coiled like snail shells; some were curved like candy canes. One of the largest was *Endoceras*, which sported an 11-foot-long (3.4 m), spear-like body, making it maybe the most fearsome

PLECTRONOCERAS

predator of its day. At only about 8 to 10 inches (20 to 25 cm) wide, modern species of nautilus aren't quite so terrifying. They live deep in the Pacific Ocean, where they scavenge the seafloor for food.

ENDOCERAS

Early shelled cephalopods, like ellesmerocerids, plectronoceras, and endoceras, came in many shapes and sizes. The earliest nautiloids had straight shells, but in the Ordovician they began to diversify: some had squat shells like pyramids, and others were curved or rounded. Some swam horizontally, others vertically, and may have alternated swimming with walking along the bottom of the ocean.

AMPHICYROCERAS

Lots and lots of stuff filled the oceans. And many of the creatures that rose up during this time are still around today. The relatives of the first starfish, called crinoids, showed up, looking like small daisies on the bottom of the ocean. Seashell-type animals called brachiopods and mollusks spread into thousands of new species. There were only a few reefs in the Cambrian, but they flourished in the warm, shallow seas of the Ordovician and gave homes to lots of algae, sponges, and other creatures. Like fish!

The first fish had evolved at some point in the Cambrian but became widespread in the Ordovician with a group called the Pteraspidomorphi. They were small, but they were a huge step forward for life: the first vertebrates! What we first saw in the nerve cord of the *Pikaia* (see page 48) had now evolved into a backbone. This series of bones connected by cartilage gives animals strong protection of their spinal nerve while still permitting a wide variety of movement. Backbones were a trait that permitted animals to grow much larger, and they set the stage for everything from dinosaurs to whales to humans.

Pteraspidomorphs were heavily armored, especially on their large heads. They presumably needed protection because they were bottom-feeders, focused on vacuuming morsels off the seafloor rather than keeping an eye out for predators. There aren't any of these little guys around these days. Their closest relatives are the hagfish and lampreys, which evolved away from having a backbone and are now more eel-like.

Life really spread out in the Ordovician. Animals left the seafloor and explored new habitats. Some ventured into the different depths of the ocean, some burrowed into the mud and muck on the bottom of the sea, and some were finally inching onto land.

Plants started in the oceans with everything else, as tiny single-celled organisms called algae. There's lots of algae still on Earth today. Algae is found in all kinds of bodies of water, either still as single-celled little guys or as big strands of seaweed or even bigger forests of kelp. It's *all* algae.

But at some point that algae started creeping up out of the ocean and onto land. It was probably around in tidal areas—where it would be underwater half the time and out of water the other half—more than a billion years ago. Over many millions of years, it's thought that some of the tidal algae evolved into plants that could spend their whole lives on dry land. Scientists don't know a ton about it because all they really have for fossil evidence are spores—tiny cells used by plants for reproduction—found in rock. They've figured out that those earliest land plants were probably mosslike ground cover, similar to a plant we have today called liverwort. These land plants actually played a role in what came next—a major mass extinction.

It was the second-largest mass extinction in the entire history of the planet with about 80 percent of all species on Earth going extinct. Scientists are still working out exactly what caused the Ordovician extinction, but they believe there were a number of factors.

There was a lot of carbon dioxide gas in the atmosphere at that time. (Today, the concentration of carbon dioxide is around 412 parts per million, which is more than ten times *lower* than levels during the Ordovician period.) Carbon dioxide heats the planet up, so the early Ordovician seas were warm. Then some large volcanic eruptions flooded parts of Earth's surface with a kind of lava that became a rock called basalt when it cooled. Basalt sucks carbon dioxide out of the air. And as that happened, things started getting colder.

While carbon dioxide was being soaked up by basalt, plants helped by breaking rocks down and exposing the chemicals inside them to the air. This took even *more* carbon dioxide out of the atmosphere. It was getting colder and colder, and the drop in temperature resulted in a lot of species going extinct.

The dropping temperatures caused glaciers to form at the South Pole. The glaciers grew and grew, sucking up a lot of seawater to form the ice. Sea levels around the world dropped, leaving many of the shallow seas—and the species that lived there—high and dry. Many more species died out after this change in sea levels, in a second wave of the extinction. And that was the end of the Ordovician.

After a few million years, carbon dioxide levels began to rise again, the glaciers receded, and the Silurian period began. The Silurian was quick, as far as geological time goes—only 26 million years of relative peace and quiet.

There was some cool new life that developed in the Silurian. The first vascular plants to ever exist were formed here. *Vascular* means that these plants could transport water and nutrients throughout their bodies, in the same way that modern trees carry nutrients up from their roots. These plants, from the *Cooksonia* genus, didn't have roots, though. They were the most advanced plants on land at that time, but they were still clustered near water.

Part of the reason it took plants a while to spread to the interior of the continents was because the land was pretty rocky. There wasn't much good dirt to grow in. But help was on the way! Fungi, bacteria, and small plants added to the natural forces of wind and rain to break down some of those rocks and improve the soil, which encouraged larger plants to grow. Eventually . . .

The supercontinent Gondwana was still the major continent at the time. A peninsula jutting off the edge near the equator will eventually become what we now know as Australia. Most of the rest of Gondwana covered the South Pole and much of the southern part of Earth's surface. Out there, across what was called the Paleo-Tethys Ocean, were a few other small continents, like Laurentia, Baltica, and Siberia. Things were relatively close together, and so most of the northern half of the globe was a huge ocean called Panthalassa.

Panthalasssssaaaa. It basically means "all over ocean" in Greek. And that's where a lot of the action in the Silurian was happening.

Down on the seafloor, a community of lampshells and other shelled brachiopods lived in large colonies, sometimes as part of coral reefs. Some huge reefs formed during the Silurian in the shallow sea that covered what is now the Great Lakes of North America.

EXPLAINED! **CORAL REEF**

Corals are little soft-bodied animals that attach themselves to something and stay there. They pull little bits of food out of the water as it flows by. To defend themselves against being eaten, many corals produce hard skeletons made out of calcium, the same thing that makes your bones hard and strong. When thousands and millions of those corals live together, they can produce huge structures on the seafloor, known as **coral reefs**, which then attract other animals looking for food or places to hide. Coral reefs become bustling underwater cities, home to millions of creatures of all kinds.

Silurian reefs facilitated the growth of tons of new species, including some of the earliest representatives of what would become sea slugs, snails, sea lilies, and feather stars. Trilobites were still cruising around, too, plus lots of different shellfish, including large water-filtering colonies of lampshells, small *Cardiola* clams, and many others. But the real stars were . . .

New fish! Lots of new fish!

Yes, new fish. Let's start with the acanthodians, also known as spiny sharks. They're not technically sharks despite looking similar to them. They were mostly made of cartilage, an elastic kind of body tissue that you humans have connecting your bones. It makes it easier for spiny sharks (and actual sharks) to swim quickly through the water. An important thing acanthodians had evolved was a jaw with teeth that could open and close. Prior fish just had roundish mouths that they used to suck up food.

Another new fish was the placoderm! They were tanks—heavily armored predators that patrolled the seafloor.

They started small—the species *Entelognathus primordialis* was only about 8 inches (20 cm) long. But some placoderms would eventually grow to be more than 30 feet (10 m) long! Huge, bone-faced killer predators!

There were larger predators around, too, like *Megamastax*! They grew to more than

three feet (1 m) long and had a huge mouth that could crush hard-bodied animals, like bone-headed Galeaspida fish.

There were also fish like *Guiyu oneiros*, one of the earliest bony fish ever found! While most of the fish before the Silurian were primarily made of cartilage, other fish with bony skeletons evolved during this time, and they paved the way for many of the more familiar fish living in waters around the world today.

So many fish, Earth, life is really cranking!

 Yup, the Silurian had a lot going on underwater, but it wasn't even the biggest time for fish. That'd be our next stop, the Devonian, which was also known as the Age of Fishes!

Well that's convenient, because I think fish are my favorite!

Really, Pencil? We haven't even gotten to the big stuff yet.

Oh. I guess we'd better keep going. On to the Devonian!

CHAPTER 6

WHEN PLANTS KILLED EVERYTHING

The Devonian Period

> It's so nice to finally have trees! I haven't been in the shade this whole time. I think my eraser is sunburned!

> Yeah, trees and plants were great until they killed everything.

> Trees…killed everything?

> Yep, but first let's go meet some cool fish.

The Devonian started 419 million years ago and lasted for 60 million years.

Earth's continents were coming together. Laurentia and Baltica had smashed into each other during the Silurian and formed Euramerica. And the large continent of Gondwana was drifting toward Euramerica, setting the stage for another supercontinent: Pangaea. (We'll get there.) The Devonian was a warm time, so there was little ice and high sea levels. The land masses were still pretty cramped together, and everything else was that massive ocean, Panthalassa.

Overall, it was a pretty calm time. Which meant that life could continue bursting into every nook and cranny and habitat and environment on the planet.

A giant called *Jaekelopterus*, an arthropod, was almost 9 feet (2.7 m) long! Remember the arthropods? They're the

phylum that today includes insects and crabs. Well, *Jaekelopterus* may have been the largest arthropod that ever lived! This creature was a type of eurypterid. Also known as sea scorpions, eurypterids' large and powerful bodies helped them flourish during the Silurian and Devonian ages. They were fast and nimble predators, and they probably hunted fish in shallow water.

Now it's fish time! The primitive jawless fish that had dominated the Silurian were evolving into more diverse families of jawed fish. Some of the more advanced fish ate plants or small animals. The *Bothriolepis*, an armor-plated bottom-dweller, fed on small invertebrates and decomposing plant material. Yummy!

Titanichthys was an armored fish like the *Bothriolepis*, but massive—sometimes more than 16 feet (4.9 m) long. They were gentle giants, though, and they survived by gulping down small fish or filtering small animals out of the water, like some whales do today.

There were also predators around. *Holoptychius* evolved round scales to help it slide quickly through the water after prey.

Cheirolepis developed large eyes to help it hunt—they were especially useful in murky freshwater lakes.

Also hunting in freshwater was the massive *Rhizodus*, which, at more than 20 feet (6.1 m) long, is the largest freshwater fish ever known. They may have even fed on sharks. That's pretty serious.

But it also means there were sharks! *Cladoselache* were the first true sharks, and they looked a lot like some of the species still swimming in oceans today. Just like modern sharks, they had sleek bodies that allowed them to speed through the water after agile prey.

But neither those sharks nor the *Rhizodus* were the most fearsome marine predators during the Devonian. Not even close! That was *Dunkleosteus*! About 10 different species of this type of fish have been found, including ones that were 30 feet (9 m) long. Instead of teeth, they had bony plates that they could slam down with more force than a *Tyrannosaurus rex*! Their powerful bites allowed them to crunch through armored prey, like ammonites with their tough shells, or even armored fish.

As fish started moving into shallower waters to find food, they started coming in close contact with both solid ground and the air. Fish fins started to be used as legs of sorts, pushing along the mud instead of swimming. There wasn't much oxygen in the water of some of the small ponds and swamps, so some species developed lungs to be able to get oxygen from the air. These fish became the earliest four-limbed animals. They weren't really fish at all anymore but rather tetrapods, a group that now includes everything from mice to cheetahs to humans.

The plants and mosses and bacteria and algae that had crept onto dry land during the Silurian continued to do their work turning the barren rocks into nutrient-rich dirt, or soil, in the Devonian.

Once there was some soil to hang out in, arthropods fully left the water and began to live entirely on land. What might have been the first-ever insect, *Rhyniognatha hirsti*, hung out up there. Scientists know very little about it because only a small part of its body has been found, but it may have had wings and looked something like a modern-day mayfly.

Plants grew larger and into evolved new forms. *Archaeopteris* plants were likely the first trees. Following millions of years when plants only grew a few inches high, *Archaeopteris* could grow to 80 feet (24 m) or more.

EXPLAINED! TREES

At the end of the day, **trees** are just big plants. Their stem grows strong to help them grow tall—it becomes a wooden trunk. Roots spread out underground for stabilization and to bring water and nutrients up into the tree. Branches reach out from the trunk with leaves or needles to photosynthesize sunlight into energy that the tree needs to grow. Trees can be all sizes and shapes, including the largest tree on Earth, the 250-foot (76.2 m) tall Giant Sequoia. There are billions of trees on Earth, and they are critical to keeping our climate in balance by absorbing carbon dioxide from the air and releasing oxygen for us, and the rest of life on Earth, to breathe.

Plants need water and sunlight to survive. Moving onto land was a problem for a lot of plants because they were far away from reliable water sources. But plants in the Devonian evolved new systems to prevent them from drying out, including special pores on their outsides and a waterproof outer layer to reduce water loss. Root systems helped plants reach for new sources of water underground. Once they were free from needing to be right near water, plants could go anywhere.

And so they went everywhere. Shrubby plants called lycophytes, small horsetails, ferns, and other plants swept across the continents. Plants didn't have many predators yet, so entire forests grew quickly. The dense vessels that plants used to transport water and nutrients through their bodies became strong—they became wood. This allowed plants to grow taller and taller, competing with one another for sunlight. By the end of the Devonian, plants had developed the ability to reproduce by seeds, which are more efficient and heartier than spores. Earth turned green!

Green's a good color on you.

It was a good time there for a while, but it sort of backfired. All that lush greenery was actually a primary driver of one of the largest mass extinctions I've ever experienced.

There were actually several different events covering the last 20 to 25 million years of the Devonian that resulted in this mass extinction, and scientists continue to debate the exact reasons. Plants caused major changes, lowering global temperatures and pulling oxygen out of the oceans.

Remember, plants take in carbon dioxide and sunlight and convert them to sugar and oxygen. They use the sugar for food and release the oxygen back into the air. So when Earth's surface became covered in plants, the atmosphere started to have a whole lot less carbon dioxide in it and a whole lot more oxygen. Just like the atmosphere lost a whole lot of carbon dioxide in the Ordovician, when basalt rocks sucked it up, now it was happening because of plants.

Earth got colder as the Devonian continued. Glaciers formed, pulling in water and lowering sea levels everywhere. Much of the new marine life, including many of the fish and the huge coral reefs, had thrived in shallow waters, but lower water left them stranded. The armored placoderm fish went extinct, and many other groups, like the trilobites, nautiloids, and brachiopods, lost huge numbers of species.

Plants also contributed to the extinctions in other ways. Remember how plants moving onto land helped break up rocks and create soil in the

Devonian? Well, rainwater washed a lot of that new soil into rivers and then into the ocean, where microscopic algae fed on the soil's nutrients and minerals. Those tiny algae plants blossomed in the oceans. They turned huge areas of the ocean green and used up a lot of the oxygen in the water, making it hard for other creatures to breathe, so they died away.

But there were probably other causes, too. There were some asteroid impacts—there's a huge crater, called the Siljan Ring, visible in the middle of what's now Sweden, that dates to around this time. The volcanoes might have played a role, too. By the end of the Devonian, about 75 percent of all species had gone extinct, and most of them were creatures in the water. But just as with the massive extinction between the Ordovician and Silurian periods and the extinctions that came later, the loss of certain species opened up opportunities for life to evolve in new and different directions. In our next stop, the Carboniferous period, life took a huge—and literal—step forward.

CHAPTER 7

GOOD LIVING AND THE GREAT DYING

The Carboniferous and Permian Periods

 Hey, do you know how long humans have been around?

Hmm. A few million years, maybe?

 Nope! Only about 300,000 years! We won't get to them until the end of the story! We're in the Carboniferous period now, which saw the rise of a lot of new kinds of animals, like amphibians and reptiles. Thousands of other species emerged and have existed for much longer than humans.

FORMATION OF THE EARTH

CENOZOIC ERA

YOU ARE HERE

MESOZOIC ERA   PALEOZOIC ERA

The Carboniferous period began 359 million years ago and lasted 60 million years. Earth's tectonic plates were still sliding all over the place like a bunch of wet bumper cars. A few smaller continents had collided back in the Silurian period to form Laurasia, which itself began drifting south toward the supercontinent of Gondwana. They met during the early Carboniferous, smashing into each other and forming huge mountain ranges—like the Appalachian Mountains, which still exist in the eastern United States. The newly formed supercontinent was called Pangaea.

The early Carboniferous was warm and wet. Much of the land was covered in humid swamps and tropical rainforests, and all that plant life filled the air with a lot of oxygen. And oxygen was good for animals like huge insects.

You know how the insects you see today are all pretty small? Well, part of the reason is that insects don't absorb oxygen very well. But oxygen levels during the Carboniferous were much higher than they are today, so insects had more oxygen to use to grow bigger. And grow they did!

Arthropleura was a millipede that, at 8 feet (2.4 m) long, was the largest arthropod that has ever crept or crawled on Earth. It probably had no predators when it lived, and it was a plant eater.

Another giant insect, *Meganeura*, is related to modern-day dragonflies. It was the largest flying insect in history, with a wingspan of more than 2 feet (0.61 m), or more than five times bigger than the wingspan of the largest modern dragonfly. *Meganeura* was a predator, and it chased down other insects and maybe even some land-living vertebrates.

Though there were only a couple different kinds of insects during the Devonian, there were more than a hundred in the Carboniferous. There were flying insects that looked like our modern-day damselflies, and there were cockroaches twice the size of any living in North America today. But as more insects appeared on land, other creatures ventured out of the water to eat them.

Some of the air-breathing tetrapods that evolved in the Devonian survived the mass extinction and continued evolving in the Carboniferous to spend more and more time away from the water to find food. Their bodies became stronger to help them lift themselves up on land, and their skin grew tougher to stop them from drying out. Eventually they went through enough changes that they became a whole new kind of animal: amphibians. There were no other vertebrates living on land, and so amphibians had the run of the place, evolving by the end of the period into many more species of all sizes and shapes.

EXPLAINED!

This diverse family of creatures includes modern-day frogs, salamanders, newts, and more. They evolved after fish and before reptiles, and they have elements of both, seemingly just as at home on land as they are in the water. But there are a few things that make an amphibian unique. They lay soft, jellylike eggs, like the masses of frog eggs you might see in a spring pond. They start their lives in the water, and then many of them undergo big changes as they grow up, such as changing from squirmy tadpoles into four-legged frogs. Finally, amphibians have special skin that helps them absorb oxygen from water, meaning they don't need to float to the surface to breathe.

The *Cochleosaurus* evolved during this time from an order of creatures called Temnospondyli that were likely some of the earliest amphibians. Temnospondyli grew into all kinds of different amphibian-like animals, including ones that looked like salamanders, snakes, eels, or crocodiles. The *Cochleosaurus* was one of the larger ones, at more than 5 feet (1.5 m) long, and it looked and probably acted a lot like modern crocodiles.

The warm, wet conditions in the early Carboniferous were ideal for the development of insects and amphibians, but they didn't last forever. Over the course of only a few thousand years, around 307 million years ago, the Carboniferous climate dried out significantly in what is called the Carboniferous rainforest collapse. The causes of the collapse are unclear, though they might have had to do with volcanic eruptions changing the atmosphere. Regardless of the reason, the effect was that the world cooled down and things dried out. Amphibians suffered because there was less water around for them to lay their eggs in, and the loss of oxygen-producing forests meant that it was harder for large insects to survive.

But of the many kinds of amphibians that evolved during the early Carboniferous, some had grown to spend more time away from water. These animals could travel farther in search of food, though like all amphibians, they still needed to lay their eggs in water. If amphibians were able to lay eggs on land, they would have an advantage. Then they could travel even farther in search of food, and they might also have a better chance of surviving in times of drought. Sure enough, some animals began to lay hard-shelled eggs—eggs that could be laid on land without drying out—about 310 million years ago. These creatures weren't really amphibians anymore. Scientists call them amniotes, and they were the ancestors of everything from reptiles to mammals to birds.

By the end of the Carboniferous, there were a lot of amniotes around laying these new hard-shelled eggs. Many of them looked pretty indistinguishable from modern-day lizards. But they weren't actually reptiles yet. Scientists divide the amniotes into two types: synapsids and sauropsids. These two groups were very closely related but evolved a key difference: the number of openings in their skull behind their eyes, where certain jaw muscles attached. Synapsids have one hole, and sauropsids have two. It was a small difference that eventually had huge repercussions: over millions of years, the synapsids became mammals, and the sauropsids became reptiles, including dinosaurs and, eventually, birds.

EXPLAINED! REPTILES

One of the most noticeable things about **reptiles** is their skin: it's covered in either scales or bony plates—think of the smooth scales of a snake or the tough, leathery skin of an alligator. Reptiles' tough skin helps keep water inside their bodies, allowing them to live on land instead of near the water like their amphibian cousins. A big difference between reptiles and mammals is that reptiles are cold-blooded, meaning they need to warm their bodies from the heat of the sun. That's why you commonly see snakes and lizards sunning themselves on rocks, and it's also why few reptiles are found in cold climates.

Let's meet some of the coolest representatives of the two groups. The *Edaphosaurus*—a synapsid—was a plant eater that could grow to more than 11 feet (3.4 m) long and had a fancy sail on its back. Scientists aren't really sure what the sail was for. Maybe it was to regulate body heat; maybe it was for defense; maybe it was to show off to potential mates. But it looked cool.

The *Hylonomus*—a sauropsid—is the oldest reptile known to scientists. Despite being more than 310 million years old, it looked very similar to our modern lizards, like skinks or anoles. This 10-inch (25 cm) critter hunted insects, just like its modern relatives.

Ever since their emergence in the Carboniferous, the descendants of sauropsids and synapsids have ruled the Earth. The descendants of the sauropsids, including the dinosaurs, were at the top of the food chain for millions of years, until many of them went extinct after a huge asteroid hit Earth in the Cretaceous period. (We'll get to that on page 138.) Afterward, descendants of the synapsids, the mammals, took over as the dominant group on Earth. (We'll get to that, too, on page 142.) We'll get to all that soon, but remember that it started here in the Carboniferous.

New life was evolving elsewhere. There were some cool new fish in the Carboniferous, but sharks really stole the show. Those armored fish from earlier periods, the placoderms, had disappeared at the end of the Devonian, meaning there was lots of room in the oceans. Surviving sharks could now take over some of the roles once filled by the placoderms. In the Carboniferous, sharks evolved into more than 45 different families in just a few million years, many more types of shark than there are today.

Many of these new sharks had really cool features. *Stethacanthus* were only a couple feet (60 cm) long, but they had flat-topped fins on their back that were covered in spines, like some kind of hairbrush. They had the spines on their heads, too. There's nothing like it in modern-day fish, and scientists think those spiny fins were probably used, somehow, to attract a mate.

Males of another shark species, *Falcatus*, sported a sword-looking fin sticking out over the top of their heads. This was also likely some sort of mating thing.

And then there was *Edestus giganteus*, the scissor-toothed shark. Shark teeth are constantly growing to stay sharp. The old teeth of modern sharks fall out of their mouths  when new teeth come in. *Edestus giganteus* sharks didn't shed their teeth, though. Instead, new teeth growing in their mouths pushed the old teeth forward until they were this protruding whirl of razors. Scary stuff!

SHARKS ARE SO COOL!

WHAT DRIVES EVOLUTION?

Animals evolve in all kinds of ways and for many different reasons. Here are some factors that drive change:

Safety—It's a dangerous world, and so many species evolve defenses. For example, porcupines have spines, moths are camouflaged, and antelope can run quickly away from predators.

Food—Every living thing needs to eat, and species evolve in all kinds of ways to help keep themselves fed. Giraffes evolved long necks to help them reach leaves that no other animals were eating. Finches evolved strong bills to help them crack open seeds.

Attracting a Mate—You're not going to pass your genes along if you can't attract a mate, and animals have evolved in all kinds of interesting ways to impress the opposite sex. Antlers let male deer show how big and strong they are. A male bird's beautiful song lets females know that it's strong enough to sing loudly and that it has a good territory.

Isolation—Animals separated from one another, such as by living on islands, often have a different experience than those living on the mainland. Sometimes a lack of food causes species to become smaller than their mainland relatives, such as with certain species of dwarf chameleon on islands off Madagascar. Other species may get bigger on islands, typically when there are fewer predators around. Many New Zealand bird species are examples of this phenomenon, and so is the dodo, a giant pigeon that used to live on the island of Mauritius. These "islands" don't need to be oceanic islands but can be any area cut off from its surroundings, including freshwater lakes cut off from the ocean, mountaintops, grasslands that divide forested areas, and other geographic features.

As the supercontinent of Pangaea continued to drift south at the end of the Carboniferous, glaciers formed and another ice age took hold. Earth was cold through the beginning of the Permian period about 300 million years ago, but it began to warm up a few million years in. By the middle of the Permian, about 275 million years ago, Earth was downright hot, and in the wake of the Carboniferous rainforest collapse, the interior of Pangaea had turned from swampy forests to one of the largest deserts to ever exist.

The lack of water, which helped drive the evolution of amniotes from amphibians in the Carboniferous, continued to drive evolution in the Permian. The planet's earliest plants reproduced via spores—tiny, unprotected one-celled reproductive units usually carried by the wind to a spot where they can grow into new plants. But some plants evolved stronger, more reliable reproductive units—seeds—in the Devonian, millions of years before the Permian. Plants with seeds, like early conifer trees, had better success in the dry conditions of the Permian, and they spread widely. Some of the trees that evolved during the Permian, like conifers, ginkgoes, and palm tree–like cycads, are still around today.

The animals really got wild in the Permian period. Remember how at the end of the Carboniferous, the stage was set for the sauropsids that became reptiles and the synapsids that became mammals to battle it out? Well, the battle heated up during the Permian.

ICE AGES

The Earth fluctuates between periods where there are large sheets of ice at the poles—**ice ages**—and times when the poles are free of ice—greenhouse periods. Global temperatures change for different reasons, but the Earth is warmer when there are more chemicals in the air that work to trap the Sun's heat in Earth's atmosphere, such as carbon dioxide, and cooler when there are more chemicals in the air that allow the Sun's heat to escape Earth's atmosphere, such as oxygen. Living in an ice age doesn't necessarily mean that the whole world is frozen, though. In fact, the Earth is currently in an ice age that began about 2.5 million years ago: the Quaternary glaciation.

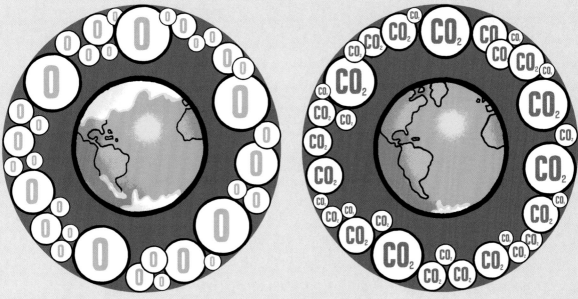

ICE AGE GREENHOUSE PERIOD

Let's begin with the mammal-like synapsids. Here's a classic: *Dimetrodon*. These were bigger versions of the *Edaphosaurus* from the Carboniferous period, and they were no longer plant eaters but carnivores. At as much as 15 feet (4.6 m) long, they were one of the top predators of the early part of the Permian. Dimetrodons were part of a family called Sphenacodontidae, which made up about half of the mammal-like lizards at this point.

EXPLAINED! MAMMALS

Humans are **mammals**, but so are things that are definitely not humans, like whales and tigers and mice. So what do mammals all have in common? A few things: The bodies of all female mammals produce milk to feed their babies. Mammals all have fur or hair, rather than scales or feathers (even whales have a few hairs). They all have three bones in their ears to help them hear, and they also all have a special area of the brain called a neocortex, which helps them perform more complex mental tasks than other animals, including, for humans, language.

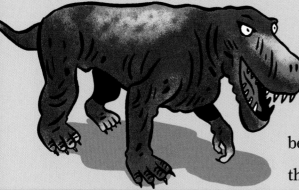

Another major group of mammal-like synapsids was the therapsids, the dominant Permian predators. The *Gorgonops* was a kind of crocodile-bear with huge teeth perfect for ripping through the toughest skin of its prey.

The *Pristerognathus* was dog-sized but had a huge, long head and jaws that could open really wide.

Not all the therapsids were giant predators, though. A *Diictodon* was a plant eater that built elaborate burrows in the desert to stay safe and cool.

These therapsids and others began to show more mammalian traits. Some evolved fur, which helped keep them warm, and sensitive whiskers that could be used to detect prey in the dark, allowing smaller therapsids to hunt safely at night. Some therapsids evolved to have their legs underneath them, like dogs, rather than out to the side, like crocodiles, which helped them run faster.

Elsewhere, the sauropsids, the reptile-like things that became actual reptiles, were evolving into their own unique shapes.

One group of these were the parareptiles. The parareptile *Bunostegos* was like a big, armored lizard-cow. Like cows, these knobby-faced giants were herbivores—plant eaters—and likely grazed on small plants in some of the drier parts of Pangaea.

Another group of sauropsids that emerged toward the end of the Permian were creatures like *Archosaurus*, which probably looked a lot more like modern crocodiles, and they spent their time in the water ambushing prey. This group would eventually flourish, becoming dinosaurs, pterosaurs, crocodilians, and birds.

EXPLAINED! MASS EXTINCTIONS

The Earth changes, and sometimes those changes have drastic impacts on living things. When changes cause lots of living things to go extinct, scientists may call it a **mass extinction**. These events can occur for many reasons, including major volcanic eruptions, asteroid impacts, or changes in oxygen levels. Scientists debate the official number of mass extinctions in Earth's history but think there have been around 20 events in the past 540 million years. That's not that many, really! Mass extinction is a scary thing to think about, but life on Earth has survived each one in some form. In fact, extinctions can open the door to lots of new life to develop. Evolution helps life bounce back, better than ever.

 We're about to get to the "Great Dying." It was hard to watch. I was so excited by all these new creatures crawling and swimming all over me, and then . . . they were gone. About 96 percent of all species in the oceans went extinct, as well as 70 percent of all land animals and many insects.

The Permian–Triassic extinction wasn't that much different from the major extinctions that came before it. It was just *worse*. So we're about 250 million years in the past and things were going fine, but then there was a massive volcanic eruption. It happened in the area that's now Siberia, in Russia, and this eruption is known as the Siberian Traps.

It was bad. There was molten rock covering an area maybe as large as the entire United States, and huge plumes of ash and dust, which blocked out the Sun and caused deadly acid rain. The eruptions also released carbon dioxide, which you now know heats up the planet. Even worse, remember how all those swampy forests had dried out millions of years earlier? Well, the loss of all those forests resulted in a lot of dead plants, which, over the years, were buried under rocks and pressed into a new rock called coal. Coal is flammable. The Permian eruptions ignited some of that coal, which caused huge fires and released millions more tons of carbon dioxide into the air, warming the Earth up even further. Humans today burn coal to make heat and electricity, and its emissions are part of what is warming the present-day climate.

All the carbon dioxide in the air resulted in less oxygen in the water, killing lots of marine life and causing lots of another chemical, hydrogen sulfide, to rise out of the oceans and into the atmosphere. It poisoned plants and animals on land. It was a really sad, rough couple million years on Earth.

EXPLAINED! COAL

Coal is dead plant matter that has been buried underground then squeezed and heated over millions of years until it becomes rock. Humans dug up coal and found that it burns, just like a log burns on a campfire, and that coal could be used to create heat and, later, electricity. Coal has been an important source of energy for many years, but it is falling out of favor because of its impact on the environment. Coal must be dug out of the ground, which can cause destruction to the surrounding areas. Burning coal releases the carbon dioxide stored in the plants, which contributes to global warming. Instead of coal, humans today are focusing on clean, renewable sources of energy like solar, wind, and geothermal.

But life went on, didn't it, Earth?

It sure did. That cycle of loss and then growth happens all the time in my history.

CHAPTER 8

KING LIZARD TIME

The Triassic and Jurassic Periods

Dinosaurs are probably the most famous group of extinct animals that ever lived, but to me they're just one of the many amazing groups of creatures that have called me home.

Yeah? You don't pick favorites?

Oh, who am I kidding? Dinosaurs and other massive Triassic and Jurassic reptiles were *so awesome*! Long necks! Sharp teeth! Underwater hunters! I can't wait to show them all to you!

FORMATION OF THE EARTH

CENOZOIC ERA

YOU ARE HERE

MESOZOIC ERA   PALEOZOIC ERA

t's King Lizard Time! The Triassic period was the first part of a new era, the Mesozoic. The Permian extinction killed a whole lot of things, but not everything, and the creatures that survived flourished. Many of those creatures were reptiles, and the Triassic is when they began their takeover.

The Triassic began 251 million years ago and lasted for 50 million years. Most of the land on Earth's surface at this time was part of Pangaea. The Tethys Ocean filled the gulf in the C-shaped part of the supercontinent, and the rest of Earth's surface was covered in that huge ocean, Panthalassa.

It took millions of years for life to recover from the Great Dying. Scientists who study rock formations know this because there isn't any coal found from the early Triassic, which means that there weren't many plants around to die and turn into coal.

Some creatures survived. In the ocean, clams, snails, and crabs survived and flourished. On land, the *Lystrosaurus*, an odd, shovel-faced therapsid (one of the synapsids, the reptile-like things that became mammals), survived the extinction and found itself virtually without predators in southern Pangaea. It had  the complete run of the place: Scientists estimate that at one point in the early Triassic, *Lystrosaurus* made up about 95 percent of all advanced life on land. No other group of animals has ever done that.

Amphibians almost went entirely extinct, but the few that survived bounced back pretty quickly, such as the semiaquatic trematosaurs and capitosaurs. There were also some sauropsids (the reptile-like things that became reptiles), in addition to the synapsids  (the reptile-like things that became mammals). The mammal-like synapsids had outnumbered the reptile-like sauropsids in the Permian, but that changed in the Triassic.

No one is exactly sure how it happened, but at some point, sauropsids, specifically a group called the archosaurs, became the dominant creatures on Earth. Archosaurs include extinct groups like dinosaurs and pterosaurs, and they also include modern-day birds and crocodiles.

Pterosaurs were the first noninsects to fly. Their once lizard-looking front feet evolved a very long fourth finger, which held out a thin membrane: a wing. With a long tail to help them steer, they became accomplished fliers. In time, they evolved into many different forms and ranged in size from the 10-inch (25 cm) *Nemicolopterus* to the 40-foot (12.2 m) *Quetzalcoatlus*!

Another type of archosaur that evolved during this time was the dinosaur. *Eoraptor* was one of the earliest known dinosaurs. It was only a few feet (1 m) long, but it had several adaptations characteristic of later dinosaurs, like the ability to walk on two legs.

A long tail helped it balance, and strong legs helped it run fast while still freeing up its two front legs to act as arms. Eventually some dinosaurs would evolve back onto four legs, but they began on two. We're going to spend a lot more time with dinosaurs later, so let's get to everything else in the Triassic first.

Ichthyosaurs started out as land-living reptiles with four legs. But the seas were pretty empty at the beginning of the Triassic, so these creatures didn't have much competition for food in the oceans. They spent more and more time in the water, and eventually their legs evolved into flippers to help them swim. Their tails evolved into tails like those that sharks or whales have, to power them along underwater. They evolved from walking creatures to swimming creatures.

But hadn't things already evolved from *swimming* things to *walking* things? Those first tetrapods?

Yes! Evolution doesn't just work in one direction. Animals evolve to fit into whatever environments are available to them.

I see! My understanding of evolution is . . . evolving.

Once back underwater, reptiles took on still more shapes. There were some that looked like sea serpents, like *Cymbospondylus*.

Others were almost identical to modern dolphins, including *Stenopterygius*, and were incredibly fast swimmers and hunters. Still others became huge, like the *Shastasaurus*, which was around 70 feet (21.3 m) long and probably hunted squid by sucking them into their toothless jaws.

114

But these weren't the only reptiles that came back into the ocean. Another separate group of reptiles also evolved back into swimming predators, becoming the plesiosaurs. Instead of evolving to look like fish or whales, plesiosaurs looked like nothing that exists now—they were flat-bodied with wide flippers and very long necks. Some were slow-moving ambush hunters, while other species grew large and became the dominant predators in the oceans of the Jurassic.

Not all reptiles in the Triassic time were crazy sea monsters or early dinosaurs. Some were early versions of things we know, like turtles! This is *Proganochelys*. Its ancestors slowly evolved a set of expanded bones across their backs, which provided a layer of protection from predators. By the time of *Proganochelys*, those bones had become a shell that was similar to the shells still sported by modern turtles.

PROGANOCHELYS

And some of the mammal-like reptiles at the time were becoming just plain mammals! As reptiles were getting larger, many smaller creatures needed to find ways to avoid becoming their lunch. The most successful of them, like the *Megazostrodon*, became small and nocturnal. During a time when most predators were active during the day, these early mammals played it safe by only coming out at night and spending their days safely hidden in underground burrows.

MEGAZOSTRODON

Becoming nighttime hunters meant some big changes for mammals. For example, the temperature of reptile bodies changes with the

temperature around them. They're cold-
blooded, which is why you see snakes
or alligators basking in the sun to warm
up. But because there isn't any sunlight in
the middle of the night, mammals needed
another way to stay warm. So they evolved to
become warm-blooded, meaning they kept a constant body temperature
by developing the ability to gain heat from the food they eat.

EOZOSTRODON

Mammals also developed fur and hair to help them stay warm, and
because it was so hard to see in the dark, their eyesight and senses of
hearing and smell improved to help them live under the cover of darkness.
Some of the ways that mammals evolved to
survive in a reptilian world eventually
protected them from the things that
killed off the dinosaurs and allowed
mammals to dominate the present day.

ADELOBASILEUS

PANGAEA

Before we get to the Jurassic period and those showstoppers—the dinosaurs!—there is yet another mass extinction. (I know, there've been so many extinctions.) This time, about 76 percent of all species on Earth died out. The causes of the extinction are, again, not really clear. Volcanoes, as usual, likely played a major part. The plates were moving again, making the supercontinent of Pangaea split apart toward the end of the Triassic, and all that stress caused some huge eruptions in the middle of the continent. The volcanoes probably caused the climate to change, heating up the planet, causing the oceans to become more acidic, and once more causing lots of creatures to go extinct.

Just like at the end of the Permian, oceanic species were hit particularly hard by a rapid change in the water quality in the oceans. Many species of underwater snails, clams, and oysters went extinct, as did an entire group of eel-like creatures called the conodonts. Many of the marine reptiles didn't make it out of the Triassic. On land, almost half of all tetrapods went extinct, including many species of the large Temnospondyli amphibians we met back in the Carboniferous. Lots of other different kinds of early reptiles were lost, too, like the aetosaurs and the rauisuchids. But many creatures squeaked through, including turtles, crocodiles, fish, those little early mammals, and, of course, the dinosaurs, who would find themselves with a lot of room to roam in the Jurassic.

The Jurassic period was 201 million years ago, after the Triassic extinction ended, and it lasted for 56 million years. The supercontinent of Pangaea continued to break apart, leaving two new continents: Laurasia in the north, which included what are now North America, Europe, and Asia; and in the south, Gondwana, made up of what are now South America, Africa, Antarctica, and Australia. The coastlines of some of the modern continents took shape as the continents continued to drift. What is now western Africa split from today's eastern United States. Australia was getting ready to pop off Antarctica, and around the world the general shapes of today's continents were beginning to show themselves.

The climate was warm. Some areas were dry, and others were humid and, because plants grow most densely in wet areas, covered in jungle. Plant life was pretty similar to that in the Triassic, dominated by pine trees, ferns, palmlike cycads, and ginkgoes.

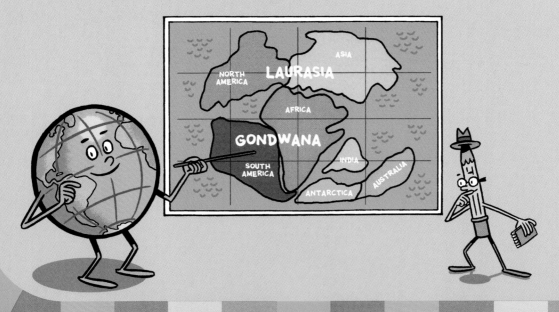

I know you're really excited about dinosaurs, but there was a lot more to the Jurassic than just giant reptiles. We're going to start small and work our way up! A new insect appeared. It's an *Archaeolepis* moth, one of a group of insects that have colorful scales on their wings and long tubular snouts for drinking water. The descendants of these insects would

become even more colorful and eventually begin using their snouts to drink nectar from flowers: in other words, they'd become butterflies.

There were predators around, too, like *Juramaia*. Barely bigger than a mouse, this mammal skulked around the Jurassic, maybe at night, hunting insects. It needed to skulk and stay out of sight because it had predators of its own, like *Archaeopteryx*.

Archaeopteryx is a dinosaur! It might not be the first dinosaur that jumps to mind, but it helps show that dinosaurs came in all sizes and shapes. Generally, dinosaurs were reptiles with their legs underneath them—not out to the sides like crocodiles or modified into wings or flippers like flying or marine reptiles. Some dinosaurs walked on four legs, some on two. Some were big, and some were tiny; some ate meat, and others ate plants. Some, like *Archaeopteryx*, had feathers. Scientists are just now understanding that many more dinosaurs had feathers than we used to think. Feathers most likely evolved from reptile scales to help keep smaller dinosaurs warm or to let them put on colorful displays for potential mates. Dinosaurs like *Archaeopteryx* and others found that these new feathers were useful for gliding, and they made short flights among the treetops. This was safer than having to come down to the ground. Over millions of years, these gliding reptiles turned into the modern, diverse, and beloved birds we know now.

DINOSAURS TO BIRDS

Dinosaurs evolved into all kinds of species, including the mighty *Diplodocus* and the ferocious *Tyrannosaurus rex*. Other dinosaurs evolved into something else completely: birds. Long, fluffy feathers may first have evolved to help keep dinosaurs warm or as colorful decoration to show off to potential mates. *Archaeopteryx* is the earliest known dinosaur to use them for another purpose: flying. There were flying reptiles at the time called pterosaurs, who had evolved wings made of skin. Like the pterosaurs, flying helped *Archaeopteryx* move quickly in order to find food and likely helped them avoid predators by staying off the ground. It was a successful strategy, and over millions of years feathered dinosaurs evolved to get even better at flying. Their heavy jaws evolved into a light beak, they lost their long reptile tails, and their bones became hollow to save weight. Several lines of modern birds lived alongside the dinosaurs, including the ancestors of modern ostriches, ducks, geese, and chickens. A few of these birds survived the extinction that killed the dinosaurs and evolved into the more than 10,000 bird species alive today.

> Lots of new life evolved after the dinosaurs went extinct, huh?

 Yup! Birds and mammals had a lot more room to expand.

There were larger dinosaurs around, too, of course, like the fearsome *Allosaurus*. It wasn't quite as large as the *Tyrannosaurus*, but both walked on two legs, had small arms, and had huge skulls with teeth like saw blades for shearing meat. At more than 30 feet (9 m) long, *Allosaurus* was the top predator of its time. It ate basically whatever it could catch.

Stegosaurus was a plant eater with massive plates on its back and a dangerous spiked tail. It was like a heavily armored cow. Scientists aren't exactly sure what the plates on its back were for—either to help regulate heat or to defend against predators like *Allosaurus*, or possibly something else. That tail, though, was definitely for defense.

Sauropods were a group that included absolutely gigantic dinosaurs, the largest creatures ever to walk on Earth's surface.

One Jurassic species, *Supersaurus*, has been estimated at 115 feet (35 m) long, longer than the biggest modern whales. Some sauropods stood more upright and were extremely tall. *Sauroposeidon* was the size of three giraffes standing on top of one another. There have never been walking creatures as long, heavy, or tall as these dinosaurs in Earth's entire history.

The size of the sauropods helped them reach food that no other animals could reach, similar to modern giraffes. But it was also for protection. Not even the meanest predatory dinosaur could take down a full-grown sauropod, and many species had long tails that may have been employed as whips for defense. There were many different species of sauropods, but they were all plant eaters who generally stayed in wet or coastal habitats.

After so many billions of years with slow and steady growth, life was absolutely everywhere in the Jurassic. Dinosaurs, marine reptiles, birds, insects, amphibians, mammals, fish…I was JAM-PACKED WITH LIFE!

CHAPTER 9

THE OTHER BIG BANG

The Cretaceous Period

> We've got some more dinosaurs to get to here in the Cretaceous.

> This is a big-time dinosaur era. I've seen the movies, I'm ready!

> It was a fun period. Nice weather…lots of continents moving around…big, cool animals. Ended badly, that's for sure. But it was fun while it lasted.

The Cretaceous lasted a good 79 million years, from about 145 million years ago to 66 million years ago. The warm weather from the Jurassic continued in the Cretaceous. There was no ice to suck up extra water, so the sea levels were high. The large continents of Laurasia and Gondwana continued to split apart and began to look like the continents we know today, just with a lot more water on them. For example, what is now the United States had a large, shallow ocean covering the Southeast and Midwest. It was called the Western Interior Seaway, and it split the continent into two halves.

The Cretaceous was absolutely teeming with all kinds of cool creatures. For example, the *Quetzalcoatlus*! We first met pterosaurs back in the Triassic, but over many millions of years they got bigger and bigger. These reptiles had 40-foot (12 m) wingspans, which is larger than some airplanes. *Quetzalcoatlus* pterosaurs were amazing predators, but they probably didn't hunt much from the air. Instead, they had evolved to be very comfortable on the ground, and like modern-day herons or storks, they probably hunted small animals.

The seas were overflowing with big, hungry creatures. There were lots of sharks still around, though after a few extinction events they weren't quite as diverse as they had been in their heyday during the Carboniferous. *Cretoxyrhina* sharks were 25 feet (7.6 m) long and pretty much exactly like giant great white sharks.

Styxosaurus were massive 35-foot-long (10.6 m) plesiosaurs, another type of creature we met back in the Triassic period. About half of their length was made up of their incredibly long necks. They mostly ate fish.

Tylosaurus were 40 feet (12.2 m) of hungry reptile, and though they

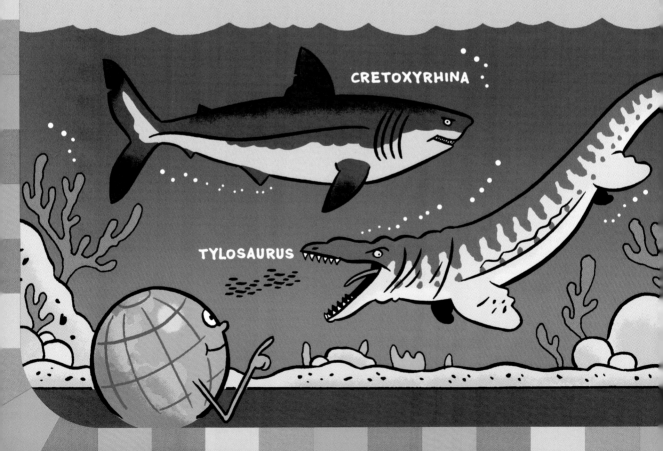

CRETOXYRHINA

TYLOSAURUS

looked like some of the other sea creatures we've seen in Earth's history, they're from the family of mosasaurs, which are more closely related to snakes than sharks.

The oceans were wild during the Cretaceous. Things were eating and trying not to be eaten. In addition to those huge lizards, there were 20-foot-long (6.1 m) *Xiphactinus* fish, bigger than any bony fish currently swimming around in the oceans. There were huge sea turtles, like the 15-foot (4.5 m), 5,000-pound (2,200 kg) *Archelon*. There were even marine birds! *Hesperornis* was a 6-foot-long (1.8 m) flightless bird built for catching fish underwater, like a cross between a penguin and a loon.

STYXOSAURUS

ARCHELON

XIPHACTINUS

It's hard to say the exact moment when birdlike dinosaurs became actual birds, but their evolution continued from the Jurassic, and by the end of the Cretaceous, some of the birds we know today started to appear. It was beneficial for these dinosaurs to be as light as possible, as lighter birds could climb more easily and, eventually, fly. Their bodies lost their typical dinosaur tail, which was made of bones, and replaced it with feathers. Their heavy, bony jaws evolved into lightweight beaks. In other words, they became birds. One of them was *Vegavis iaai*, a large bird that may have looked and sounded like modern geese. Few other fossils of Cretaceous birds have been found, but scientists studying bird DNA understand that the ancestors of different kinds of modern birds had already evolved during the Cretaceous, including shorebirds, chickens, parrots, and songbirds.

Believe it or not, there were very few flowers on Earth until the Jurassic, and they flourished during the Cretaceous. Reproduction is a challenge for plants because they're stuck in one place—they can't move around to find a mate. Up until this point, the wind helped pollinate most plants by carrying reproductive material called spores from one plant to another. This is still how many plants, like conifers, pollinate.

But eventually, plants evolved to recruit animals to help them pollinate. What most likely happened is that a mutation in a leaf made it appear interesting to certain insects, like wasps. The wasp investigated the leaf, got some pollen on its back, and carried it to another part of the plant, achieving pollination. Plants started producing all kinds of colorful, nice-smelling, nectar-providing flowers to attract insects to help them move pollen from one place to another.

EXPLAINED! POLLINATION

New plants don't just come out of nowhere! Just like humans and many other life-forms, plants reproduce by combining the genetic information from one plant with the genetic information of another plant. Flowers produce **pollen**, which is carried by the wind or by an animal—most famously bees, but also moths, bats, reptiles, birds, bears, and many other creatures—into flowers from another plant. Once there, the pollen produces sperm, which fertilizes the flower, turning first into a seed and then into a new plant.

The Cretaceous was a big time for plants as well as for plant eaters. *Triceratops* was the most famous member of the group of beaked, horn-faced, and frill-headed dinosaurs called the ceratopsids. The biggest of them were more than 30 feet (9.1 m) long, much of that made up of their massive heads. Their horns and giant, bony frills likely served the same purpose that deer antlers or ram horns serve today: to show their strength and attract a mate.

THE OTHER BIG BANG

Each ceratopsid species deployed its own combination of horn and frill. *Chasmosaurus* had small horns and a heart-shaped frill. *Styracosaurus* had a single horn, like a rhinoceros, with spikes jutting out from the tops of its frill. *Pentaceratops* had an extra-tall frill covered in little horns. Males would battle with their horns and show off their fancy frills to impress females. Their frills were also likely used for defense from other dinosaurs.

Tyrannosaurus rex was the most fearsome of hunters. It was a member of a group of dinosaurs called the theropods, which had hollow bones and generally walked on two legs. The earliest theropods are the direct ancestors of birds. But another branch of the theropods, the one that included *T. rex*, evolved to be some of the most fearsome hunters ever to walk on Earth.

T. rex had large eyes, a wide skull, and a narrow snout, giving it better vision than modern humans—perfect for hunting prey. It's estimated that *T. rex* had the strongest bite of any land animal, ever. Other theropods included the *Allosaurus*, from back in the Jurassic, and the even bigger *Giganotosaurus*.

Neither *T. rex* nor *Giganotosaurus* was the biggest theropod predator around, though. That honor goes to *Spinosaurus*, an unbeatable

60-foot-long (18.3 m) predator with a giant fin on its back. It had a long snout like a crocodile and a long eel-like tail that helped it swim. In fact, *Spinosaurus* is one of the only dinosaurs that is known to have been a swimmer. It probably inhabited waters a lot like those where modern crocodiles live.

With all those massive dinosaur predators around, smaller animals had to figure out how to survive. A small, rodent-like mammal called *Meniscoessus* burrowed underground for safety. There, *Meniscoessus* and other mammals could hide during the day and venture out under cover of night to search for food.

There were a lot of mammals around in the Cretaceous, from mouse-sized ones to beaver-sized ones. Some lived in trees, like opossums, while some spent most of their time in the water, like otters. Others were ratlike and spent a lot of time underground or in dense vegetation.

The ways in which Cretaceous mammals adapted to hide from dinosaurs ended up helping them survive a much bigger threat: a mass extinction.

Things were going along fine 66 million years ago. Dinosaurs were walking around on land, marine reptiles were swimming in the seas, and pterosaurs were flying through the skies. Then: an asteroid hit.

You remember how Earth used to get hit by asteroids all the time, way back in the Hadean? It still happens today, actually—thousands of meteors enter Earth's atmosphere each day, but most of them burn up before they hit the ground. Rocks large enough to make it to Earth's surface can do damage, and really big ones can cause a worldwide catastrophe.

The asteroid that ended the Cretaceous was between 6 and 9 miles (9.6 and 14.4 km) wide. No one knew it was coming, but it smashed into the area that is now eastern Mexico with unimaginable force.

There were both immediate and long-term effects from the asteroid impact, and scientists are still trying to piece together exactly what happened after the asteroid struck. There is general agreement that there was near-immediate destruction in the area around the impact. A shock wave and air blast is thought to have flattened forests for as much as 1,100 miles (1,770 km) around. Gigantic tsunamis, with waves 325 feet (99 m) tall, smashed across the coastlines of what is now the Caribbean and North America. Immense earthquakes radiated from the impact site.

As devastating as these impacts were, however, they weren't enough to cause a massive worldwide extinction. Other theories attempt to understand what happened in the days and months after the asteroid hit. One theory suggests that things got very hot, very quickly, as the billions of tons of earth, sand, and debris that the asteroid kicked up into the atmosphere burned up as they fell back to Earth. The heat given off by those billions of tons of debris as they fell would have been enough to raise the temperature on Earth's surface to more than 1,000°F (538°C), causing worldwide fires and killing much of the life on Earth.

Other theories suggest that it took longer for the extinctions to occur. A massive cloud of dust kicked up by the impact is believed to have lingered in the air for more than a year, blocking out all sunlight. Without the sun, organisms that relied on sunlight for photosynthesis, like marine plants and algae, died out. Then so did any marine creatures that ate the plants or algae, and then the things that ate them, too. Chemicals in the dust mixed with clouds and fell back to Earth as toxic acid rain, which killed more animals in the ocean. Entire food chains collapsed. Oceanic species, from the smallest shelled mollusks to huge, predatory plesiosaurs, were gone.

Scientists estimate that about 75 percent of all species disappeared after that asteroid. That's a lot. But it also means that 25 percent of them survived. It seems crazy that anything could have made it through, but they did. The deepest parts of the ocean, where there isn't much sunlight anyway, weren't impacted all that much, so some fish and sharks and other marine animals survived.

Creatures on land that survived the initial impact, either by hiding out in underground burrows or in other safe places, then faced the challenge of finding food in a totally changed landscape. Many plant eaters perished—there were no more plants to eat. But creatures that ate dead things, such as insects that ate decaying plants, and the creatures that ate those insects, could find their way through.

Mammals and birds survived. So did crocodiles and turtles and amphibians and ferns and trees. Lots of life made it through and into the Cenozoic era—the one *you* live in now.

CHAPTER 10

YOU ARE HERE

The Cenozoic Era

> We're in the homestretch now—almost at present day.

> Wait, really? We're going from dinosaurs straight to humans?

> No, not straight to humans. First we've got to see gigantic three-horned rhinos, megapredators with hooves like a pig, tiny mammals that became ocean giants, and elephants covered in hair. *Then* we get to humans.

YOU ARE HERE

FORMATION OF THE EARTH

CENOZOIC ERA

MESOZOIC ERA   PALEOZOIC ERA

t took a long time for things to bounce back after the asteroid impact that ended the Cretaceous. Though the climate only took about 10 years or so to return to normal once all the dust settled and the fires went out, it took more than 10 *million* years for plant and animal diversity to return to pre-asteroid levels.

The mammals we met underground in the Cretaceous eventually emerged and found few predators and lots of room to roam.

PLATYPUS

HORSE

MONKEY

APE

KANGAROO

Though they were mostly small and rodent-like in the days of the dinosaur, mammals began to evolve into all kinds of new shapes and sizes in the Cenozoic. Ancestors of modern mammals began to appear, including groups that would become everything from sloths to deer to kangaroos. There were also all kinds of other mammals, too, ones that aren't around today—mammals that were as big and as fierce as any dinosaur. We'll meet them all here in the Cenozoic, the Age of Mammals.

The mammals that survived the asteroid found themselves in a world largely empty of other animals, and so they rapidly diversified into many different body types and lifestyles. Some of them got huge. The 3-ton (2.7 t) *Megacerops* looked like a giant, double-horned rhinoceros. *Arsinoitherium* was another two-horned beast, 10 feet (3 m) long and 6 feet (1.8 m) tall; it evolved from the same ancestors as elephants. Other relatives of elephants, woolly mammoths and mastodons, had thick coats of hair that kept them warm in cold, northern climates. They lived until only a few thousand years ago, eventually undone by a warming climate and human hunters.

Different giants evolved in what is now South America, which was an island unconnected to North America until some

PARACERATHERIUM

WOOLLY MAMMOTH

MEGACEROPS

time between 3 million and 15 million years ago. The biggest species there were massive sloths, relatives of the slow-moving jungle species of today. *Megatherium* was more than 20 feet (6.1 m) long and weighed as much as an elephant. Meanwhile, the eight-foot (2.4 m) *Thalassocnus* sloth had adapted to a semiaquatic life, using its sharp claws to hold itself underwater as it grazed on algae or grass.

But the largest mammal to ever stomp around on Earth's surface was *Paraceratherium*. It belonged to a now-extinct family of mammals closely related to horses and rhinoceroses, and it lived in the forests of what is now western Asia. It was taller than a giraffe and four times as heavy as a modern elephant.

MEGATHERIUM

Just as with the dinosaurs, where there are large plant-eating animals, there are large meat-eating animals to hunt them. Many different types of predators evolved during the Cenozoic, including the ancestors of our modern mammalian predators, like cats, dogs, and bears.

Sarkastodon was a 10-foot-long (3 m) megapredator and an early relative of lions and wolves. It likely preyed on the largest land mammals of the time. Its family, the Oxyaenidae, went extinct more than 30 million years ago. Many of the Oxyaenids' relatives survived, though, and diversified into other predators, like *Smilodon* and other saber-toothed cats, on their way to becoming modern big cats.

Other Cenozoic predators had more unusual relatives. A family of mammals called the mesonychids looked like wolves, and some were larger than modern bears, but they had hooves. Some mammals evolved hooves— basically overgrown toenails

that protected the feet and allowed the animal to run quickly on hard surfaces—early after the end of the dinosaurs, and their ancestors live on as horses, deer, antelope, and others. But hooved mammals were once more varied and included *Andrewsarchus*, the largest land-living mammalian predator of all time, twice the size of a polar bear!

EXPLAINED! FOOD WEBS

Energy and nutrients move through an ecosystem by a complex system of things-eating-other-things, called a **food web**. Understanding food webs helps us understand how different plants and animals are connected and how they affect each other. For example, a leaf takes in energy from sunlight and nutrients from the ground. An insect eats that leaf for food, and then a mouse eats the insect. The mouse is eaten by an apex predator, a falcon, which then returns nutrients to the soil in its waste, which is used again by another leaf. Food webs help us understand that if something happens to the leaf, the whole system may get thrown out of balance, eventually impacting the insect, the mouse, and the falcon.

During the Cenozoic, the continents were sliding into their modern places. Things almost looked pretty much like the present day.

Did you know the continents are still moving? No one knows for sure what's going to happen, but at the rate things are going, in 250 million years everything may have combined again into a giant supercontinent.

I can't wait to see that!

Mammals were flourishing on land, and some of them even began venturing into the water.

Indohyus may have been among the first, about 50 million years ago. This raccoon-sized mammal looked like a regular land mammal, but it spent a lot of time in the water and evolved some special traits to help it stay underwater. *Indohyus* and their descendants and relatives continued to move deeper into the seas and continued to evolve bodies that made swimming easier. Bones became heavier

and less buoyant. Feet evolved into fins. Tails became flat to help propel the animals underwater. Only about 10 million years after *Indohyus* was dipping its feet in the water, its relatives, the basilosaurids, were fully recognizable as modern whales. They eventually evolved into all modern whales, including the largest animal ever to have existed on Earth, the blue whale at a length of 98 feet (29.9 m) long.

And remember sharks? From way back in the Silurian? Well, they're still here, of course. They survived everything. The biggest and baddest of them all were the megalodons. These guys made great whites look like goldfish. They were almost 60 feet (18.3 m) long, with teeth the size of a man's hand, and they *ate whales*. There were some other large animals in the oceans, mostly other large whales that also ate other whales, but nothing was as fearsome as the megalodons.

One very special mammal during this time was *Altiatlasius*, a small creature that climbed among the trees about 50 million years ago. It turns out that climbing nimbly through trees was a pretty successful way to live in the Cenozoic, and after millions of years of evolution, *Altiatlasius* and its relatives gave rise to a whole bunch of newer tree-dwelling animals: primates, a group that includes monkeys, lemurs, and great apes.

Many of those primates looked and acted like the monkeys and great apes around today, walking on all fours, covered in hair, and living in or near trees. But one group of apes living in what is now eastern Africa underwent a small but incredibly important shift: they stood up. Ape skeletons are not designed to stand on just two feet, but standing

up has some important advantages. Hands could now be used to carry things or reach up high. Standing up made it easier to spot predators, and it was easier to run away or to chase after prey. Over time, this group of apes evolved skeletons that made standing and walking and running easier, and somewhere between 4 million and 6 million years ago, apes like *Australopithecus* were completely bipedal (on two feet).

Once their hands were free, these bipedal apes found so much to do with them. At least 3 million years ago, some of the descendants of the earliest walking apes began to use tools. A group of these apes, called *Homo*, developed hands with improved flexibility, and they used them to wield stone tools. Large, sharp stones could be used to cut meat, separate animal

hides, cut wood, and dig up plants.
When combined with another
technological milestone—
harnessing fire—these apes,
now more appropriately called
early humans, could cook their
food and keep warm.

As the use of tools allowed them to eat better, early humans underwent
another important change: their brains grew. Operating a big brain
requires a lot of energy, but now that more food was available, thanks to
better tools and hunting techniques, they could spare the extra calories.
Plus, there was a lot to learn. These early apes likely always hung out in
groups, but their relationships were getting more complex. They were
developing language, teaching hunting and tool-making skills, and
learning to live together in groups. Larger and more complex brains
helped them do all of these things.

As early humans evolved, they moved around. Their ability to catch
and eat many different foods and to keep themselves warm and safe
allowed early humans to explore new habitats and areas. Starting about
200,000 years ago, early humans began leaving Africa, first spreading
into what is now the Middle East, India, Europe, and Asia. Then, just

15,000 years ago, they traveled along a thin piece of land that connected to Alaska and down into North America and South America. Humans had conquered the globe.

And they didn't stop learning. About 50,000 years ago, early human societies began to act in ways that no other animal ever has. They began to make art, creating images on cave walls of the animals around them. They buried their dead. They painted their bodies and wore jewelry, and they made increasingly complex tools. Around 11,000 years ago—just the tiniest sliver of a blink of an eye in Earth's history—humans learned how to plant crops and domesticate animals, and soon they no longer needed to follow migrating animal herds and could instead stay in one place.

With permanent homes came villages, and then towns and then cities and streets. They made books to read and toys to play with and school buses to ride. And they made it all the way to right now where you are reading this book!

 What a great story!

It's *your* story, Earth. Thank *you* for letting us all be part of it.

Final Notes from Interview with
EARTH

What an incredible conversation with Planet Earth. I learned so much. But then I wondered, what happens next? What's in store for Earth and the plants and animals that live on it?

At some point, probably around 5 billion years in the future, the Sun will change. It's currently in its most stable phase as a star, churning through billions of years of hydrogen fuel. But eventually the Sun will run out of hydrogen, at which point it'll grow so big it will overtake the Earth and the other planets in our solar system. But that won't happen for a long, long time.

Things are expected to be pretty much the same on Earth for now. Tectonic plates will keep sliding around and banging into one another, causing new continents and mountain ranges and oceans to form.

Over millions of years, the Earth will continue cycles of heating and cooling, and those cycles, as well as any unforeseen events, may impact life on Earth as they have before. Existing species may disappear, and then, eventually, new species will evolve to replace them.

In fact, humans are causing some of those impacts already. The Earth has never seen a species like humans before, with their technology and their brains and their ability to grow and survive. A side effect from all the amazing things humans are doing is that they're changing the planet, and in doing so, they're hurting other plants and animals.

Humans are taking over natural areas to build towns and cities, leaving fewer places for other animals to live. Humans are polluting the air and water, making it harder for other animals to survive.

And, perhaps most urgently, humans are causing the planet to warm up. I learned from talking with Earth that times when the planet rapidly heats or cools can mean hard times for life on Earth, and humans are currently causing the planet to warm up much faster than normal. If humans don't figure out how to reduce their impact on the planet, lots of species may go extinct: The speed that we're causing our planet to warm is faster than the speed at which humans and other species can adapt. If global temperatures were rising at a more gradual rate, many species would have time to adapt their behaviors or their habitats to fit into the changing world. But humans are causing things to change too quickly, and many species are being left behind. If humans don't figure out how to reduce their impact on the planet, lots of species may go extinct.

Humans have caused lots of species to go extinct already, beginning thousands of years ago, when overhunting likely contributed to the extinction of mammoths, mastodons, South American giant sloths, and massive dome-shelled glyptodonts. In just the past few hundred years, species like the great auk, the Caribbean monk seal, and the Tasmanian tiger have all been made extinct. The passenger pigeon may have once been the most numerous bird on Earth, with flocks so big over the eastern United States that they blocked out the Sun. But humans hunted them and destroyed their habitat, and now there are no more passenger pigeons alive.

Earth described major extinctions throughout its history and showed us that it took millions of years in each case for life to return again. Today, scientists worry that humans may be causing another major extinction on Earth. If that's true, it may take millions more years for life to flourish again.

But it doesn't have to be that way. In just the past hundred or so years, humans have woken up to the impacts they're having on the Earth, and many of them are working to make things better. There are lots and lots of ways to help, and the Earth needs everyone working together. You can start right in your home, by recycling, eating locally grown foods, and planting native plants in your garden. You can take larger actions, too, like convincing governments to protect more wild lands, build renewable energy, reduce plastic waste and other pollution, and work on many more issues.

There's lots to be done, and thankfully, humans are smart. They don't want to ruin their home, and they want to live in a place with other plants and animals. If humans work together, they can solve the problems they're causing and make life easier for themselves and for other plants and animals. If they can do that, life on Earth has a very bright future.

 I can't wait to see what it will be like!

HOW YOU CAN PROTECT EARTH'S FUTURE

The Earth needs all the help it can get to stay clean and healthy. Here's how you can help!

1 DON'T USE A PLASTIC STRAW AT LUNCH.

Plastic products are convenient, but once you throw them away they can stay in the trash for hundreds of years. Instead, drink from a reusable straw!

2 WALK OR RIDE YOUR BIKE INSTEAD OF RIDING IN THE CAR.

Much of the pollution that is causing climate change comes from the burning of fossil fuels, like the gasoline that powers most cars and trucks. If you can, walking, biking, or taking public transportation is healthier for you and for the Earth.

3 LEAVE YOUR LEAVES!

Raking up leaves in the fall is hard work, so leave them if you can! Many beneficial insects like butterflies and worms live underneath the leaf litter, protected from the winter cold. Keeping leaves on the ground saves insects, and your back!

④ EASY WAYS TO PROTECT BIRDS.

Cats and windows are very dangerous to birds. Cats hunt birds outside, and birds mistakenly fly into windows that reflect the sky or habitat. Scientists estimate that cats and windows kill more more than 3 billion birds per year! You can help by keeping your cats indoors and putting stickers, screens, or special tape on the outside of your windows.

⑤ TURN OFF THE LIGHTS!

Your parents probably remind you all the time, but they're right: lights, TVs, phone chargers, and other electric gizmos use electricity. By turning things off when you're not using them, you can save electricity and save money.

⑥ PICK UP TRASH IN YOUR NEIGHBORHOOD.

Litter looks bad and can be harmful to wildlife and the environment. Spend a day with your family and friends picking up litter and disposing of it properly. You'll be proud of how you helped make your neighborhood look!

⑦ USE FEWER CHEMICALS.

Many household cleaners and lawn-care products are full of chemicals that can harm water quality, air quality, and wildlife. Ask your parents to choose natural products at the store, and keep those chemcials out of the environment.

⑧ RECYCLE!

Instead of just throwing products into the garbage, figure out which items can be used again. Many towns have recycling programs, which take plastic bottles, aluminum cans, cardboard, and other products to special factories to be turned into new products instead of being thrown away.

⑨ JOIN UP!

There are lots of organizations that can help you learn more about the Earth, from camps to school groups to environmental nonprofits like the National Audubon Society or the Sierra Club. You can join at any age to learn more about the world and meet people who care about the same things you do.

⑩ WRITE YOUR ELECTED OFFICIALS.

Every state and town holds elections to decide who makes new laws, and it's the job of those elected officials to listen to the people they represent—and that means you! If there's an issue you care about, have an adult help you write a letter to an official—from your mayor or town council to your state legislators to federal congresspeople—telling them how you feel and asking them to vote to protect the environment.

ASK THE EARTH
Q+A

Earth told me a lot about its history, but there are still some important things that we didn't get to. I asked some kids what they wanted to know about the Earth, and here are the questions they came up with!

1 WHY IS THE SKY BLUE?

Light from the Sun actually contains all the colors of the rainbow, and each color moves at its own speed, called a wavelength. When sunlight enters our atmosphere, most of the wavelengths move right through, but the blue wavelengths are just the right size to bounce off molecules of gas in the air. The blue light bounces and scatters all around, making it more visible to our eyes, and making the sky appear blue.

2 WHAT IS THE DEEPEST PART OF THE OCEAN AND THE HIGHEST MOUNTAIN?

The planet has changed so much in its history that no one knows what the tallest mountain ever was, but the current tallest mountain on Earth is

Mount Everest, on the border of Nepal and China, at 29,032 feet (8,849 m) tall! The deepest point in the ocean is called the Challenger Deep, part of the Mariana Trench in the western Pacific Ocean, at an incredible 36,200 feet (11,033.8 m) below the surface, or almost 7 miles (11.3 km) underwater!

3 HOW DO DESERTS FORM?

Deserts are large areas of land that receive very little rain. Sometimes rain clouds are blocked by mountain ranges, like the Andes in South America or the Himalayas in Asia, which help create the Atacama and Gobi deserts. Weather patterns also bring less rain to some areas, creating many deserts around the world. The largest desert in the world is the Sahara in northern Africa, although the frozen continent of Antarctica also receives very little precipitation and could be considered a desert as well.

4 WHY ARE THE OCEANS SALTY?

If you've ever been swimming in the ocean, you know that the water is salty and not good to drink. This salt mostly comes from rocks on land. When rain falls on land, it collects tiny bits of rock and carries them with it as the water collects in streams and rivers and eventually flows into the ocean. Some saltiness also comes from cracks in the seafloor called vents, which add minerals to the water.

⑤ HOW BIG IS THE SUN?

To put it simply: the Sun is huge. More specifically, the Sun is 864,400 miles (1,391,117 km) across—more than 1.3 million Earths could fit inside the Sun! But as large as it is, our Sun is only an average-sized star. Other stars elsewhere in the universe are more than 100 times larger than our Sun!

⑥ WHAT ARE THE BIGGEST ANIMALS TO HAVE EVER LIVED?

Believe it or not, the largest animal to have ever lived on Earth is still alive today: the blue whale. This massive sea creature can reach almost 100 feet (30.48 m) long and weigh more than 30 elephants. There have been other huge creatures through time. With their long necks and tails, certain sauropod dinosaurs were longer than blue whales—up to 150 feet (45.7 m) long—but not heavier.

⑦ HOW DO CLOUDS FORM?

The reason your wet towel dries when you leave it outside is because the Sun causes water to change from a solid to a gas in a process called evaporation. Water is evaporating all the time, from lakes and puddles and oceans and pools, and the water vapor gas drifts up into the air. Cooler temperatures or lower pressure high in the atmosphere change the water vapor from a gas back into a solid—and a cloud is formed. Sometimes the tiny water droplets combine to make heavier water droplets, and when they're too heavy to stay in the air they fall to the ground as rain or snow.

8 HOW ARE RIVERS FORMED?

When rain falls on land, it either seeps into the ground or begins flowing downhill, pulled by gravity. As the water flows, it collects in low points, becoming streams, which continue flowing downhill. Many different streams collect into larger flowing waterbodies: rivers. Eventually, rivers flow into the sea. Where the flow of water is stopped by areas of high land, or a dam, a lake is formed.

9 HOW DO GLACIERS SHAPE THE EARTH?

The Earth has undergone many glacial periods throughout its history, including the current Quaternary glaciation, and each time glaciers advance or retreat, they shape the land beneath them. Glaciers are heavy—they weigh millions of tons—and they scrape up the ground beneath them as they inch along. The impacts of glaciers are seen on landscapes all around the world, from the deep, U-shaped inlets in Norway called fjords to bowl-shaped cirques carved into mountains in the Rockies, Alps, and many more.

10 WHAT IS THUNDER AND LIGHTNING?

Lightning is a massive discharge of electricity from a storm cloud to the ground, and thunder is the sound of lightning. When tiny particles of frozen water bump up against each other in clouds during certain conditions, they produce small electric charges. Those small charges can then accumulate into a massive charge, which may eventually burst toward the ground as lightning. A bolt of lightning is so quick and powerful it briefly superheats the air around it, causing it to expand and then contract, causing the loud crack of thunder.

⑪ WHAT IS A RAINBOW?

We see blue sky because blue light bounces off molecules of air (see question 1 on page 164), but sometimes we can see more colors when there's water in the air, like right after it rains. When light enters a dense water droplet, it bends as it reflects off the inside of the droplet, separating into its component colors. We see the separated colors as a rainbow. Rainbows are actually full circles, but we can usually only see half—an arc—from the ground.

⑫ WHAT CAUSES TIDES?

If you've been to the beach, you may have seen that the level of the water rises and falls during the day. Those are tides! They're caused, if you can believe it, by the gravity of the Sun and the Moon. Just as the Earth's gravity pulls on the Moon, keeping it in orbit, the Moon's gravity pulls on Earth, but less so because the Moon has less mass. The Moon pulls on our oceans as the planet rotates, causing two high tides and two low tides each day.

ALL THE TIME IN THE UNIVERSE

All planets rotate—that is, spin around in place like a figure skater—and all planets also revolve—that is, do a lap around the Sun like running around a track. On Earth, one rotation is one day, and one revolution is one year. We're used to our days and years on Earth, where daytime is when we're facing the Sun and nighttime is when we've rotated away from the Sun. We do that 365 times and it's a year. But days and years are very different on other planets, which sometimes rotate and revolve faster or slower than Earth. Venus has the longest day, at 5,832 Earth hours, and Neptune has the longest year, at more than 164 Earth years.

PLANET	ROTATION PERIOD	REVOLUTION PERIOD
MERCURY	59 EARTH DAYS	88 EARTH DAYS
VENUS	243 EARTH DAYS	225 EARTH DAYS
EARTH	1 EARTH DAY	365 EARTH DAYS
MARS	1.03 EARTH DAYS	1.88 EARTH YEARS
JUPITER	0.41 EARTH DAYS	11.86 EARTH YEARS
SATURN	0.45 EARTH DAYS	29.46 EARTH YEARS
URANUS	0.72 EARTH DAYS	84.01 EARTH YEARS
NEPTUNE	0.67 EARTH DAYS	164.79 EARTH YEARS

PRONUNCIATION GUIDE

Acanthodians
(ack-un-THO-dee-ins)

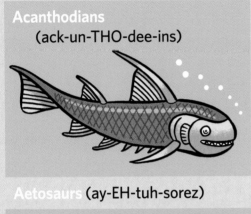

Aetosaurs (ay-EH-tuh-sorez)

Allosaurus (a-luh-SAW-ruhs)

Altiatlasius (all-tee-at-LASS-ee-us)

Amniotes (AM-nee-ohts)

Andrewsarchus
(an-droo-SAAR-kuhs)

Anomalocaris
(ah-nom-ah-lo-CAR-is)

Archaeolepis moth
(are-key-AH-leh-pis mawth)

Archaeopteris (ar-key-AP-tuh-ris)

Archaeopteryx
(aar-kee-AAP-tr-uhks)

Archean Eon
(aar-KEE-uhn EE-aan)

Archelon (AAR-chuh-laan)

Archosaurs (AR-kuh-sorez)

Archosaurus (ar-kuh-SORE-us)

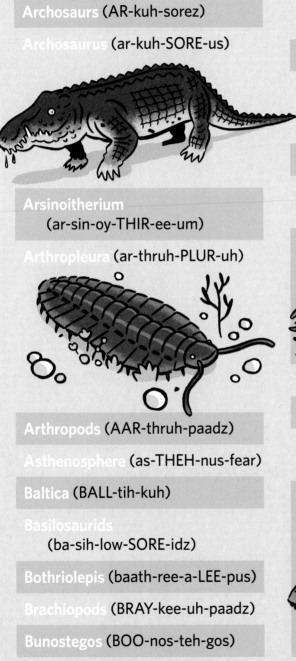

Arsinoitherium
   (ar-sin-oy-THIR-ee-um)

Arthropleura (ar-thruh-PLUR-uh)

Arthropods (AAR-thruh-paadz)

Asthenosphere (as-THEH-nus-fear)

Baltica (BALL-tih-kuh)

Basilosaurids
   (ba-sih-low-SORE-idz)

Bothriolepis (baath-ree-a-LEE-pus)

Brachiopods (BRAY-kee-uh-paadz)

Bunostegos (BOO-nos-teh-gos)

Cambrian Period
   (KAM-bree-uhn PEE-ree-uhd)

Capitosaurs (CAP-ih-to-sorez)

Carboniferous Period
   (kar-buh-NIH-fer-us
   PEE-ree-uhd)

Cardiola (car-dee-OH-lah)

Cenozoic Era
   (see-nuh-ZO-ick ER-uh)

Cephalopod (SEH-fuh-luh-paad)

Chasmosaurus (KAZ-mo-sore-us)

Cheirolepis (CARE-oh-LEP-iss)

Cladoselache
   (CLAY-doe-SELL-ah-kee)

Cochleosaurus
   (coke-lee-oh-SORE-us)

Conodonts (KO-nuh-dants)

Cooksonia (cook-SUHN-ee-ah)

Cretaceous Period
(krih-TAY-shus PEE-ree-uhd)

Cretoxyrhina (krih-tox-ee-RYE-nuh)

Crinoids (KRAI-noydz)

Cyanobacteria
(sai-a-no-bak-TEE-ree-uh)

Cycads (SAI-kadz)

Cymbospondylus
(sim-bow-SPON-dill-us)

Devonian Period
(dih-VO-ni-an PEE-ree-uhd)

Diictodon (die-ICK-toe-don)

Dimetrodon (dai-MEH-truh-daan)

Dunkleosteus (dun-kul-OS-tee-us)

Edaphosaurus
(eh-duh-fuh-SAW-ruhs)

Edestus Giganteus
(eh-DESS-tuss jai-GAN-tee-us)

Endoceras (en-DA-ser-uhs)

Entelognathus primordialis
(ent-eh-loh-NA-thous
pry-more-dee-AH-lis)

Eoraptors
(ee-oh-RAP-tors)

Eudimorphodons
(you-die-MORPH-oh-donz)

Eukaryotes (yoo-KEH-ree-oats)

Euramerica (yur-uh-MER-ih-kuh)

Eurypterid (you-RIP-tuh-rid)

Falcatus (fal-CAT-us)

Galeaspida (GA-ley-ah-spee-da)

Giganotosaurus
(jai-GAN-oh-toe-SORE-us)

Gondwana (gun-DWA-nuh)

Gorgonops (GORE-gon-ops)

Great Auk (grayt awk)

Guiyu oneiros
(GWE-you OH-nee-ros)

Hadean Eon
(HAY-dee-uhn EE-aan)

Hallucigenia
(huh-loose-ih-JEN-ee-ah)

Hesperornis (hes-puh-ROAR-nis)

Holoptychius (ho-lop-TIH-key-us)

Huronian Glaciation
(hyu-RO-nee-uhn
glay-shee-AY-shun)

Hylonomus (hi-LON-oh-mus)

Iapetus Ocean
(eye-AP-ih-tus OH-shun)

Ichthyosaurs (IK-thee-uh-sorz)

Indohyus (in-do-HI-us)

Jaekelopterus
(yee-kuh-LOP-ter-us)

Juramaia (jur-ah-MY-uh)

Marrella (mah-REL-lah)

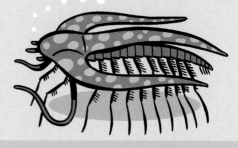

Mastodons (MA-stuh-daanz)

Megacerops (MEH-guh-ser-ops)

Jurassic Period
(jer-A-suhk PEE-ree-uhd)

Megalodon (MEH-guh-luh-daan)

Kaapvaal Craton
(KAP-val CRAY-tahn)

Megamastax
(meh-guh-MAS-tacks)

Kenorland (keh-NOR-land)

Meganeura (meh-ga-NUR-ah)

Laurasia (law-RAY-zhuh)

Megatherium
(meh-guh-THEE-ree-uhm)

Laurentia (law-REN-shuh)

Lingula (LING-guh-luh)

Megazostrodon
(MEH-guh-ZO-stroh-don)

Lithosphere (LI-thuh-sfeer)

Lycophytes (LIE-kuh-fights)

Lystrosaurus (liss-tro-SORE-us)

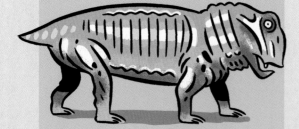

Meniscoessus (men-is-KO-sis)

Mesonychids (may-zo-NIH-key-ids)

Mesozoic (meh-suh-ZOH-ick)

Mosasaurs (MOSE-a-sores)

Nautiloids (NAH-tul-oidz)

Nautilus (NAH-tuh-luhs)

Opabinia (o-pa-BIN-ee-uh)

Opposums (uh-PAA-sumz)

Ordovician Period
(or-duh-VIH-shun PEE-ree-uhd)

Oxyaenids (OCK-see-eh-nids)

Paleo-Tethys Ocean
(PAY-lee-oh TEH-this OH-shun)

Paleontology
(pay-lee-aan-TAA-luh-jee)

Pangaea (pan-JEE-uh)

Pannotia (pa-NO-shuh)

Panthalassa (pan-thuh-LASS-uh)

Paraceratherium
(pair-ah-ser-ah-THEER-ee-um)

Parareptiles (par-ah-REP-tilez)

Pentaceratops
(pent-uh-SER-uh-tops)

Phosphorus (FAAS-fur-uhs)

Photosynthesis
(foe-toe-SIN-thuh-suhs)

Pikaia (pih-KAI-ah)

Pilbara Craton
(pill-BAR-ah CRAY-tahn)

Placoderms (PLACK-oh-derms)

Plankton (PLANGK-tin)

Plesiosaurs (PLEA-see-uh-sorez)

Pristerognathus
(PRISS-teh-ROG-nah-thuss)

Proganochelys
(pro-GAN-oh-kell-us)

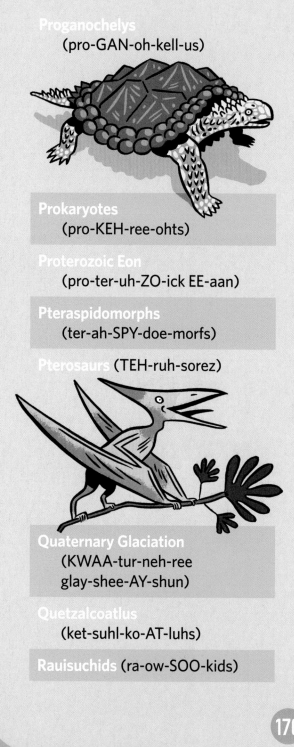

Prokaryotes
(pro-KEH-ree-ohts)

Proterozoic Eon
(pro-ter-uh-ZO-ick EE-aan)

Pteraspidomorphs
(ter-ah-SPY-doe-morfs)

Pterosaurs (TEH-ruh-sorez)

Quaternary Glaciation
(KWAA-tur-neh-ree
glay-shee-AY-shun)

Quetzalcoatlus
(ket-suhl-ko-AT-luhs)

Rauisuchids (ra-ow-SOO-kids)

Rhizodus (RYE-zo-dus)

Rhyniognatha hirsti
(rye-nee-oh-NATH-uh
HIRST-ee)

Rodinia (row-DIN-ee-uh)

Sarkastodon (sar-KAS-toe-don)

Sauropods (SORE-ruh-paadz)

Sauroposeidon
(SORE-oh-pos-i-den)

Shastasaurus (shas-tah-SORE-us)

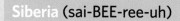

Siberia (sai-BEE-ree-uh)

Siljan Ring (SIL-ee-an ring)

Silurian Period
(sih-LUR-i-un PEE-ree-uhd)

Smilodon (SMAI-luh-daan)

Sphenacodontidae
(sfeh-na-co-DON-tih-day)

Spinosaurus (spai-no-SAW-ruhs)

Stegosaurus (steh-guh-SAW-ruhs)

Stenopterygius
(steh-NOP-teh-re-gee-us)

Stethacanthus
(steh-thah-CAN-thus)

Stromatolites (stro-MA-to-lights)

Styracosaurus
(stir-a-kuh-SORE-ruhs)

Styxosaurus (sticks-oh-SORE-us)

Supersaurus (SUE-per-sore-us)

Synapsids (sih-NAP-sidz)

Temnospondyl (tem-no-SPON-dle)

Tethys Ocean (TEH-this OH-shun)

Tetrapods (TEH-truh-paadz)

Thalassocnus (tha-la-SOCK-nus)

Therapsids (thuh-RAP-sidz)

Theropods (THEAR-uh-podz)

Titanichthys (tie-tan-ICK-theez)

Trematosaurs (tre-MAH-to-sorez)

Triassic Period
(try-A-sick PEE-ree-uhd)

Triceratops (tri-SER-uh-tops)

Trilobites (TRAI-luh-bites)

Tylosaurus (tai-low-SORE-ruhs)

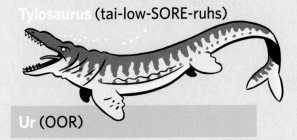

Ur (OOR)

Vaalbara (val-BAR-ah)

Vegavis iaai (VEY-gah-vis ah-ee)

Wiwaxia (wih-WAX-ee-uh)

Xiphactinus Fish
(zy-FACT-in-us fish)

FURTHER RESOURCES

BOOKS:

★ *The Ascent of Birds: How Modern Science Is Revealing Their Story*, John Reilly

★ *A Brief History of Earth: Four Billion Years in Eight Chapters*, Andrew H. Knoll

★ *Cambrian Ocean World: Ancient Sea Life of North America*, John Foster

★ *Dinosaur Facts and Figures: The Sauropods and Other Sauropodomorphs*, Rubén Molina-Pérez, Asier Larramendi, et al.

★ *Dinosaur Facts and Figures: The Theropods and Other Dinosauriformes*, Rubén Molina-Pérez, Asier Larramendi, et al.

★ *Evolution in Minutes*, Darren Naish

★ *Life Through Time: The 700-Million-Year Story of Life on Earth*, John Woodward

★ *My Encyclopedia of Very Important Dinosaurs: Discover More than 80 Prehistoric Creatures* (My Very Important Encyclopedia series), DK Publishing

★ *The Princeton Field Guide to Prehistoric Mammals* (Princeton Field Guides), Donald R. Prothero

★ *The Sibley Guide to Birds, 2nd Edition* (Sibley Guides), David Allen Sibley

★ *Space Encyclopedia: A Tour of Our Solar System and Beyond* (National Geographic Kids), David A. Aguilar, Christine Pulliam, Patricia Daniels

- *The Story of Life: A First Book about Evolution*, Catherine Barr (Author), Steve Williams (Author), Amy Husband (Illustrator)
- *Trilobite* (Extinct series), Ben Garrod (Author), Gabriel Ugueto (Illustrator)

DOCUMENTARIES:

- *The Life of Birds*, BBC
- The Planet Collection (*Blue Planet/Planet Earth/Frozen Planet*), BBC

WEBSITES:

- The National Aeronautics and Space Administration, www.nasa. gov/
- U.S. Geological Survey, www.usgs.gov/

Index

NICK LUND is a nature writer who mostly writes silly things about birds on Twitter when he should be working. His writing on birds and nature has appeared in *Audubon* magazine, *National Parks* magazine, Slate.com, the *Washington Post*, the *Maine Sportsman*, the *Portland Phoenix*, *Down East* magazine, and others. He is a graduate of the University of Maine School of Law and has worked in federal energy policy in Washington, DC, before returning to Maine with his wife and son to work for Maine Audubon.

* ⭐ * ✦

JASON FORD A diet of Tintin books, Marvel comics, and Tex Avery cartoons as a child and a continuing love of French *bande dessinée* graphic albums have contributed to Jason's approach to illustration. His drawings, incorporating juicy colors, a graphic line, and a wry wit, have kept him in constant demand. Based in London, Jason has worked for a wide range of clients and has become an author with the publication of the popular kids' activity book—*The Super Book for Superheroes* and the follow-up title, *The Monster Book of Zombies, Spooks and Ghouls*. His third title, *The Cosmic Book of Space, Aliens and Beyond*, was released in autumn 2021.